Famine

Walking In Blessing In A Time Of Famine

By

David Jones

Famine

Walking In Blessing In A Time Of Famine

By David Jones

Cover by David Jones, Faith Jones and Parry Design

© 2009 David Jones Brandon, FL.

All rights are reserved under International and Pan-American Copyright conventions. To use or reproduce any part of this book, electronically or otherwise, written permission must first be secured from the publisher. Brief quotations with credits may be used in critical review and articles.

Published by Ruach Ministries Int'l.

P.O. Box 6370

Brandon, FL 33508

Dedication

This book is dedicated to my endearing, beloved wife Faith and our wonderful children, Yakira, Joshua and Hannah. I would not have been able to finish this book if it had not been for your sacrifices and support. I truly am blessed to have you all in my life.

In Memory of

My Pastor

Bernie F. Brewster Jr.

1955-2007

Special Thanks

First, foremost and above all, I desire to thank my Savior, Messiah and Shield, Yeshua. I also would like to thank all in the congregation of Ruach Ministries International for your generous love, prayers and support. A pastor could not ask for a better congregation. I want to thank all those who gave their prayer and support, without whom this book would not be possible:

David & Darlene Jones, Linda Hinson, Alan & Eileen Westfall, Stewart & Nancy Ramey, John & Terri Davis, Pastor Curtis & Karen Taylor, Angela Kelly, Waldo & Diana Hernandez, Cliff & Natalie Skaggs, Wade Skaggs, Rachelle Skaggs, Jeanette Gomez, Richard & Alpha Cortez, Richard & Elizabeth Greenhill, Alma B. Towne, Michael & Bracha Buford, Dee Dee Russel, Doris Alfalla, Vernita Cotler, Sam & Sarah McIlwain, Yoav &Evelyn Liebovith, Georgia Martell, Kawana Richardson, Mark & Rebecca Totilo, Parry Design

And all those who wish to remain anonymous

Table of Contents

Introduction 6

Glossary of Terms 7

Chapter One
    We Are In A Famine! 9

Chapter Two
    Preparing For Famine............................. 23

Chapter Three
    What Is Your 39

Chapter Four
    Receiving From the Mouth Of God........... 55

Chapter Five
    Is The Word Burdensome? 75

Chapter Six
    The Refreshing Of The Spirit................ 101

Chapter Seven
    The River Of Refreshing....................... 139

Chapter Eight
    Walking In The Blessing....................... 159

Bibliography 195

Introduction

Deuteronomy 32:10 "He found his people in desert country, in a howling, wasted wilderness. He protected him and cared for him, guarded him like the pupil of his eye,

There are times in our lives when we feel like we are in a desert. As we look around, we may not see any relief. All of those around us are in the same wilderness that we are. At times like these it's human nature for us to question where God is. However, you have been given a divine nature by the Spirit of the living God.

Being a Pastor, I strive to approach the word in such a way that people can understand what is being said. After all, what good does it do to speak with someone and to have them not understand what you are saying? In order to get the point across that you are making, you need to be understood by those you are speaking to.

Sometimes we cannot see the answer even when it is right in front of us. There are times when we may be standing near a path but it may be difficult to see because of rough terrain. This book was written in such a way that it is easy to understand, while at the same time it reveals how to uncover the paths that we are to walk on in the wilderness.

Much like Israel in the wilderness, we have a difficult time seeing outside of our immediate situations. "Famine" will uncover why we are in a spiritual famine at this time and what can be done about it.

Glossary Of Terms

There is some terminology that will be used in this book that you may or may not be familiar with. I will list some of them here so that you will better understand what you are reading. When referring to the Name of God, I will use the names given in the Hebrew texts. I will use YHWH, Yahweh, LORD or Adonai in place of "God". I will also use Yeshua or Yahshua in place of Jesus.

The Scriptures used to quote from most often in this book is "The Hebrew Names Version". It will place a transliteration (the sounding out) of a word from the Hebrew text for certain names, words or customs. A definition of these words are as follows.

Hebrew	Definition	Hebrew	Definition
Echad	Unified one	Shabbat (Shabbatot)	Sabbath(s)
Elohim	A name for God	Shaul	The Apostle Paul
Kohen (cohen)	Priest	Tanakh	Old Testament
Kohen Gadol	High Priest	Torah	Teaching and Instruction
Matzah	Unleavened bread	Tzitzit (Tzitziyot)	Fringes
Mitzvah (Mitzvot)	Command(s)	Tziyon	Zion
Mikvah	Ritual baptism	Ya'akov	Jacob (Israel)
Moshe	Moses	Yehudah	Judah
Perushim	Pharisees	Yisrael	Israel
Ruach HaKodesh	Holy Spirit	Yitzchak	Isaac

Chapter One

WE ARE IN A FAMINE!

I am not referring to third world countries, or a recession of any kind. We are in a famine that has been prophesied by YHWH. Throughout the scriptures we see many times of famine. Abraham, Isaac and Jacob all had to face famine. Joseph had to face famine. The prophets had to face famine and hardship.

Let's face it, there are times in all of our lives when we feel that we are in a dry place. How many of us have said, or heard it said, that we feel like we are praying and listening but are not really hearing. We are in great need of rain and refreshing in our spiritual lives.

Without the rain and refreshing of the Ruach HaKodesh (Holy Spirit) we will feel dry. Without rain, rivers dry up, crops do not grow, men and animals will suffer. We need water! The same applies to our spiritual life. We need the Ruach HaKodesh (Holy Spirit) to lead us in the word so that when the times of famine come, we are prepared for it.

When you think of famine what immediately comes to mind? Websters' dictionary defines famine as;

Famine

FAM'INE, n. [L. fames.]

1. Scarcity of food; dearth; a general want of provisions sufficient for the inhabitants of a country or besieged place.

2. Want; destitution; as a famine of the word of life.

The second definition from above is what I feel to share with you in this writing.

Amos 8 defines the famine we are in at this time.

Amos 8:11-12 CJB "The time is coming," says Adonai Elohim, "when I will send famine over the land, not a famine of bread or a thirst for water, but of hearing the words of Adonai. (12) People will stagger from sea to sea and from north to east, running back and forth, seeking the word of Adonai; but they will not find it.

The famine we are in is not of food or water, even though there is a natural famine in many places all over the world today. The famine we are in is of hearing the words of the LORD. I am not saying that the word is not being proclaimed. The famine is not of proclaiming the word. The famine is of hearing the word.

To get a solid understanding of this scripture we need to understand something, the word "hear" does not mean what we may think. The Hebrew language is rich beyond one definition of a word. In Hebrew this word "hear" means more than allowing sound waves to flow to your ears. It is a process, you physically hear something, then you act on what you have heard! To hear means that you are obedient. The Strongs concordance defines this word as;

H8085

שָׁמַע

shâma'- *shaw-mah'*

A primitive root; **to hear intelligently (often with implication of attention, obedience**, etc.; causatively to *tell*, etc.): - X attentively, call (gather) together, X carefully, X certainly, consent, consider, be content, declare, X diligently, discern, give ear, (cause to, let, make to) hear (-ken, tell), X indeed, listen, make (a) noise, **(be) obedient, obey, perceive, (make a) proclaim (-ation), publish,**

regard, report, shew (forth), (make a) sound, X surely, tell, understand, whosoever [heareth], witness.

In Jewish and Messianic beliefs "Shama" is more than a word. It is a declaration, a core belief. It is a call to be obedient to the Father above all else. It is spoken three times a day. The "Shama" was heard being spoken by Jewish men as they were led to the gas chambers in World War II concentration camps. The prayer consists of three main parts, all of which is scripture. The Shema prayer is as follows;

Deuteronomy 6:4-9 CJB "Sh'ma, Yisra'el! Adonai Eloheinu, Adonai echad *[Hear, Isra'el! Adonai our God, Adonai is one]*; (5) and you are to love Adonai your God with all your heart, all your being and all your resources. (6) These words, which I am ordering you today, are to be on your heart; (7) and you are to teach them carefully to your children. You are to talk about them when you sit at home, when you are traveling on the road, when you lie down and when you get up. (8) Tie them on your hand as a sign, put them at the front of a headband around your forehead, (9) and write them on the door-frames of your house and on your gates.

Deuteronomy 11:13-21 CJB "So if you listen carefully to my mitzvot (commands) which I am giving you today, to love Adonai your God and serve him with all your heart and all your being; (14) then, *[says Adonai,]* 'I will give your land its rain at the right seasons, including the early fall rains and the late spring rains; so that you can gather in your wheat, new wine and olive oil; (15) and I will give your fields grass for your livestock; with the result that you will eat and be satisfied.' (16) But be careful not to let yourselves be seduced, so that you turn aside, serving other gods and worshipping them. (17) If you do, the anger of Adonai will blaze up against you. He will shut up the sky, so that there will be no rain. The ground will not yield its produce, and you will quickly pass away from the good land Adonai is giving you. (18) Therefore, you are to store up these words of mine in your heart and in all your being; tie them on your hand as a sign; put them at the front of a headband around your forehead; (19) teach them carefully to your children, talking about them when you sit at home, when you are traveling on the road, when you lie down and when you get up; (20) and write them on the door-frames of your house and on your gates - (21) so that you and your children will live long on the land Adonai swore to your ancestors that he would give them for as long as there is sky above the earth.

Numbers 15:37-41 CJB Adonai said to Moshe, (38) "Speak to the people of Isra'el, instructing them to make, through all their generations, tzitziyot (*tassels*) on the corners of their garments, and to put with the tzitzit on each corner a blue thread. (39) It is to be a tzitzit for you to look at and thereby remember all of Adonai's mitzvot (*commands*) and obey them, so that you won't go around wherever your own heart and eyes lead you to prostitute yourselves; (40) but it will help you remember and obey all my mitzvot and be holy for your God. (41) I am Adonai your God, who brought you out of the land of Egypt in order to be your God. I am Adonai your God."

(italics added for clarification)

The belief that this prayer is an important part of ones own belief system was not just held by the religious leaders in the time that our Savior Yeshua walked the earth. Yeshua Himself held this prayer as so important that when He was asked what the most important thing to remember was, He quoted it.

Mark 12:28-32 KJV And one of the scribes came, and having heard them reasoning together, and perceiving that he had answered them well, asked him, Which is the first commandment of all? (29) And Jesus answered him, The first of all the commandments [is], Hear, O Israel; The Lord our God is one Lord: (30) And thou shalt love the Lord thy God with all thy heart, and with all thy soul, and with all thy mind, and with all thy strength: this [is] the first commandment. (31) And the second [is] like, [namely] this, Thou shalt love thy neighbour as thyself. There is none other commandment greater than these. (32) And the scribe said unto him, Well, Master, thou hast said the truth: for there is one God; and there is none other but he:

This statement is a resounding declaration of our faith that YHWH is the one and only true God and we will serve (hear and heed), only Him! We will have no other gods or idols before Him! When we say we will hear, what we really are saying is that we will receive and do. We need to realize that as we hear the word, it helps us to increase in our faith. Furthermore, if we look at this from a Hebraic Biblical first century believer's view, since Shema involves hearing and doing, faith comes by hearing and doing the word of YHWH.

Romans 10:17 KJV So then faith [cometh] by hearing, and hearing by the word of God.

It's easy for us to say that we have faith. When it comes right down to it though, do we really? We can sit back and listen to all the sermons, worship music or Bible on CD that we can take, but if we don't act on it and allow it to change us, we don't have faith! Don't misunderstand what I am saying. We need to read the scripture. If you have it on CD or cassette, listen to it!

Once you have heard the word let it transform you and bring you closer to the One who gave us the word. Act on it! As we grow in our faith, we will grow in our love for YHWH. We will fall in love with the word like never before because it reveals our lover to us. We will fall in love with the people of YHWH, because He loves them. One thing that seems to hold true is that if our love is growing cold, so is our faith. Scripture testifies of this when Yeshua was asked about how to tell of His return.

Matthew 24:9-13 KJV Then shall they deliver you up to be afflicted, and shall kill you: and ye shall be hated of all nations for my name's sake. (10) And then shall many be offended, and shall betray one another, and shall hate one another. (11) And many false prophets shall rise, and shall deceive many. (12) And because iniquity shall abound, the love of many shall wax cold. (13) But he that shall endure unto the end, the same shall be saved.

The important thing to note here is cause and effect. Because iniquity abounds, the love of many will grow cold. In other words, they lose heart and their faith. So what does it mean to have iniquity abound? Let's look at the word iniquity. Strong's concordance lists iniquity as the Greek word:

G458

ἀ νομία

anomia - *an-om-ee'-ah*

From G459; *illegality,* that is, *violation of law* or (generally) *wickedness:* - iniquity, X transgress (-ion of) the law, unrighteousness.

In this text, iniquity equals violation of law or the transgression of the law. If we are violating the "law" that we were given to live by, we are in transgression of the law. It also notes that iniquity is unrighteousness. Which can only mean that the transgression would have to be against

YHWH, not man's law since without the word of YHWH, man cannot make righteous laws.

The only way iniquity can run rampant in our lives, is if we are unwilling to receive the word or the One who gave us the word. If we truly love the word and the One gave it to us, how difficult would it be to receive it? Once we receive the word we have the responsibility to act on it.

The famine we are living in today is by no means a lack of Bibles or scripture. I know there are many places in remote areas of the world that may not have seen a Bible as of yet. However speaking on a worldwide scale, there is not a lack of Holy Scripture, or even preachers and teachers. The time that we are in is a famine of people willing to hear the word of the LORD, receive the word of the LORD, and actually apply it to their lives and do the word. When you "DO" the word you will "BE" the word.

Our savior Yeshua HaMoshiach (Jesus the messiah) told us to go out and be the light of the world and make disciples of all men (nations) [Matthew 5:14, Matthew 28:19-20.] We should be a people set apart with the cry that David made many years ago, "thy word have I hid in my heart that I might not sin against thee."(Psalms 119:11). We may often say or quote this but do we mean it? To hide the word in our heart is to develop the close intimate relationship daily with the One who gave us everything.

If we are putting the word inside of us every day, reading it, thinking about it, talking about it, essentially living it, aren't we allowing ourselves to be changed by it? What David was talking about was getting to a place in our walk that when trials and life circumstances come our way, we need to examine how we respond. Do we respond in such a way that glorifies the Father? Through everything that happens in life, we have choices. Do we choose to respond according to our own desires or do we choose to respond according to the Fathers desire? If we allow the word to become such a part of us that it changes us, we will respond according to the heart of the Father.

Think back to when you were first learning to do something, anything. What about tying your shoes? How many of you still have to say the little story we learned in order to learn how to tie our shoes? Do you remember?

The rabbit goes around the mountain and through the rabbit hole, or something similar to that. You do not have to tell yourself how to tie your shoe, you just do it. While it is not a great spiritual revelation to learn how to tie your shoe, it is something that you will need in order to equip you for being properly dressed and going out into the world. The word of YHWH is similar to this overly simplified explanation.

As you put it into practice by doing it, you will find that it is equipping you to go out into the world and not step on something that will trip you up. You will find that the more practice you get, the easier it is to do it. You will soon see that you may not be thinking about that particular thing at all, even as you are doing it. Why? Because you KNOW it!

I am not saying do not think on the word! However, as you come to know a part of the word and are able to walk in it, do you stay there or do you move on? Let's keep moving forward and growing in the word and Spirit while cultivating our relationship with the Father.

As we get closer to our Savior, He will continue to be faithful to speak to us through His Word, and in prayer, by His Spirit. Do we spend time with Him just to be with Him, because we love and adore Him? He has given us His Word in order to show us how to walk an overcoming life in this world by His Spirit, through the building up of His body. Yeshua told us if we love Him we will do what He taught.

John 14:23-24 HNV Yeshua answered him, "If a man loves me, he will keep my word. My Father will love him, and we will come to him, and make our home with him. (24) He who doesn't love me doesn't keep my words. The word which you hear isn't mine, but the Father's who sent me.

As well, He told us that the words He taught were not His own, but that He was completely obedient to the Father and said only what He was given to say.

John 14:10 HNV Don't you believe that I am in the Father, and the Father in me? The words that I tell you, I speak not from myself; but the Father who lives in me does his works.

We will cover this more in a later chapter.

The second part of the famine that we are discussing in Amos 8:12 is; looking for the word.

Amos 8:12 CJB People will stagger from sea to sea and from north to east, running back and forth, seeking the word of Adonai; but they will not find it.

If we are looking for what we *think* is the word, instead of the Word itself, will we find it? We need to approach the Word without a preconceived idea of what we think we know. We can look all around for what <u>we</u> told the Father to give us. What do we do when we don't find it?

Are we agreeing with the word He gave us by His Spirit or are we telling God how to run our lives, and serving Him when and how we feel like it? In order to stay on the path we need to walk (or run) a steady race. When we look all over, we are running "to and fro". How much of our time, and mind, is exhausted because we need to learn how to settle down?

Have you ever helped someone look for something and you didn't know what you were looking for? If you don't know what to look for, you're going to be hard pressed to find what you need. This is a problem. There are many people today who have a void in their lives. In a manner of speaking, you could say they are spiritually hungry, have no food and worse yet, don't know where to find it.

So what is the result? They look around for whatever they can find in an effort to fill the void in their lives. We know that the need in our life is to walk in communion with the Savior, Yeshua. Now what we have is a lot of people trying to fill the void in their life with everything except what they are really searching for. We are liable to overlook or discount the very way of life that would benefit us, if we are unwilling to examine it.

Amos tells us that the famine is people not hearing and doing the word of YHWH. They will be looking for it but will not find it. How can one not hear the word, but be looking for it? Remember, earlier we defined "shama" as more than the sound waves in the air. You hear the word, receive the word, process the word, then act on it.

I feel one reason why people are looking all over to find the word but are not finding it, is that they are not willing to do what they have already been asked to do. If I come to talk to you and you tell me not now, maybe later, on a consistent basis, how much do you think I will speak to you? When the Father speaks to us by the Ruach HaKodesh or by the word, are we listening? We need to be a people seeking the true bread from Heaven.

John 6:50-51 HNV This is the bread which comes down out of heaven, that anyone may eat of it and not die. (51) I am the living bread which came down out of heaven. If anyone eats of this bread, he will live forever. Yes, the bread which I will give for the life of the world is my flesh."

If we are not willing to search for the Messiah, we will not eat the bread from heaven. We can look all over for some kind of spiritual nutritional substitute, but we won't find it. Often times the answer we really need is right under our nose.

One of the problems is that we aren't prepared for a famine when it comes. This would include people who are not willing to hear and do the word. We can sit in thousands of sermons and lectures over our lifetime and never really mature in our walk.

Are we hearing? I don't think everyone goes to their assemblies and congregations for a power nap. Don't we go with the purpose in our heart to worship? Don't we go to hear the word? Don't we go to lift up and edify our brothers and sisters?

There must be something missing in the equation. We need to "do" the word. You aren't really listening unless you are applying what you are hearing.

How many of us as parents have talked to our children and said "listen to me"? What are we saying to them? I want you to hear what I am saying and then go do what I have asked of you. Moses continually addressed this. Following the word of YHWH is not that hard.

Deuteronomy 30:11-14 HNV For this mitzvah which I command you this day, it is not too hard for you, neither is it far off. (12) It is not in heaven, that you should say, Who shall go up for us to heaven, and bring it to us, and make us to hear it, that we may do it? (13) Neither is it beyond the sea, that you should say, Who shall go over the sea for us, and bring it to us, and make us to hear it, that we may do it? (14) But the word is very near to you, in your mouth, and in your heart, that you may do it.

The problem we have in keeping the word comes in when we don't want to hear what is being said. We either discount the word by thinking it doesn't apply to us, or we convince ourselves that we don't have the problems that we do. After all, isn't it obvious that all the words of correction are for my neighbor, brother, pastor, husband, wife, etc. I want all the words of blessing and all the ones that make me feel like a spoiled child, I mean, whatever feels good to me.

What is to be done with a child who continually won't listen? Unless they change their ways, they grow up feeling everyone owes them something. In extreme cases they end up in trouble with the Law. At the core of our human nature, we want what we want when we want it. This is selfishness and pride.

We are too good to change. Everyone else has the problem. We need to see outside of ourselves and think about other people. Once we see others, we can see how to relate to them which will cause our relationships to grow.

Ironically, we look at ourselves a lot, but not in the proper way. We should examine ourselves and our thoughts, actions and relationships in order to see if we need to change. Once we change how we look at ourselves, we can go as the word said and help those who need it.

1 Corinthians 11:31-32 KJV (31) For if we would judge ourselves, we should not be judged. (32) But when we are judged, we are chastened of the Lord, that we should not be condemned with the world.

Do you realize that when you develop that close, intimate relationship that He desires with you, you are automatically going out "doing" and "being" the word of the LORD to a world that is lost and dying. You are now making disciples of all men because everywhere you go, you are spreading the light, life and love that only comes from Him! It really isn't hard to be obedient to the one you love. He gave us all that He had so that we could have everything! After all, isn't He your everything?

As we grow in our walk we will continue to understand that the things that we experience are for the knowledge of others. This is a scriptural principle addressed by Rabbi Shaul (the Apostle Paul) to the Corinthians.

1 Corinthians 10:10-11 HNV Neither grumble, as some of them also grumbled, and perished by the destroyer. (11) Now all these things happened to them by way of example, and they were written for our admonition, on whom the ends of the ages have come.

When we learn by example, we don't have to go through the same experiences someone else did. We can reap the benefit of their wisdom without the hardship. The idea here is to love the word so much, that we want to stay in it in order to know better the one who gave it to us. We should gain wisdom from the people and sages in the scripture, and their experiences, so that when the time comes to share with someone who needs to hear from their loving Father, we can help them hear.

If we don't make the investment to spend time with the Father or His word, what will we do when we need to hear from Him? We will see the importance of this in the next chapter.

NOTES

Chapter Two
Preparing For the Famine

In order to prepare for famine, we will look at how Joseph handled famine in his life. Before we get to Joseph though, we will need to lay a little foundation. We often go to Bible studies and we may or may not have an idea of what specifically we will be studying. How would you like it if you could be studying the same portion of scripture in every assembly, in every city, in every state, in every country <u>at the very same time as everyone else?</u>

Some might, at first glance, not think very highly of this. Just imagine the endless conversations that you could have. Any person you bump into on the street could be asked what they thought about what they have studied this week. Then, both of you would end up studying the word together. If the two of you, in the midst of your conversation, came across something you may not understand, you could do a "street shout out" at anyone passing by and get someone else involved in the study. We can all study the word together, and because we are all individuals who think differently and approach things in different ways, we would end up discovering new things that we may never have seen on our own.

This is the way it is in Jewish and Messianic communities. The whole word is studied in a one year cycle at the same time in every community. Imagine all the family gatherings turning into Bible studies because one person was reading something and had a question that they were not afraid or too intimidated to ask because they knew everyone else had read the same thing. This is the way it has been for thousands of years. When they did not study a yearly cycle, they studied in a three year cycle where they would cover the scriptures in a three year period.

When we study the word, we have tools to use to ensure that we are all thinking on the same passage of scripture. We know them as books, chapters and verses. Before chapters and verses, they would name the portions of scripture. The name of the passage would be one of the first few words in the passage. An example of this would be if I were to come to you and tell you I was reading in the portion of scripture "in the beginning", many of you would already know it to be Genesis 1:1. That is exactly how it worked.

The Bible is a prophetic book. Most will agree that there is a lot of prophecy contained within its covers. One thing I want to point out is how one of these prophesies tie in to what we were talking about in Amos 8:11-12. The book we call Genesis, in Hebrew would be, Beh-reh-sheit, which means in the beginning. In the book called "in the beginning" we have a portion of scripture concerning Joseph and a great famine called "miketz", which means at the end. It is recorded in Scripture that our God declares the end from the beginning.

Isaiah 46:9-10 HNV Remember the former things of old: for I am God, and there is none else; [I am] God, and there is none like me; (10) declaring the end from the beginning, and from ancient times things that are not [yet] done; saying, My counsel shall stand, and I will do all my pleasure;

We will be looking at the famine "at the beginning" in order to get a better prophetic picture of the famine in Amos 8.

Proverbs 25:2 HNV It is the glory of God to conceal a thing, but the glory of kings is to search out a matter.

The portion of scripture starts with Genesis 41:1 and goes through 44:17.

Genesis 41:1 HNV It happened at the end of two full years, that Par`oh dreamed: and behold, he stood by the river.

Pharaoh had a dream that, I believe, was sent to him by YHWH. No one could interpret what the dream(s) meant. While Pharaoh was trying to find someone who could comprehend the dreams, the Pharaoh's cupbearer remembered that while he was in prison he had a dream that Joseph interpreted.

Genesis 41:11-13 HNV We dreamed a dream in one night, I and he. We dreamed each man according to the interpretation of his dream. (12) There was with us there a young man, a Hebrew, servant to the captain of the guard, and we told him, and he interpreted to us our dreams. To each man according to his dream he interpreted. (13) It happened, as he interpreted to us, so it was: he restored me to my office, and he hanged him."

It was testified of Joseph, that not only did he have an interpretation for the dream, it was correct. There is something interesting to note here. The word used here for interpretation only occurs fourteen times in the Tanakh (Old Testament). Every time it is used, it is used in regards to Joseph. To take it one step further, it is only in chapters 40 and 41. The word for interpretation in Hebrew is;

H6622 פתר pa̒thar
to *open up, interpret (-ation, -er).*

I find it very interesting that the definition of interpret is "to open up". Joseph is a type shadow of Yeshua. Joseph said interpretations, or opening up to reveal, belongs to God, and that no one else can open up or reveal. So, what does he reveal or open up to us?

Luke 24:13-32 HNV Behold, two of them were going that very day to a village named Ammaus, which was sixty stadia from Yerushalayim. (14) They talked with each other about all of these things which had happened. (15) It happened, while they talked and questioned together, that Yeshua himself came near, and went with them. (16) But their eyes were kept from recognizing him. (17) He said to them, "What are you talking about as you walk, and are sad?" (18)

One of them, named Klofah, answered him, "Are you the only stranger in Yerushalayim who doesn't know the things which have happened there in these days?" (19) He said to them, "What things?" They said to him, "The things concerning Yeshua, the Natzri, who was a prophet mighty in deed and word before God and all the people; (20) and how the chief Kohanim and our rulers delivered him up to be condemned to death, and crucified him. (21) But we were hoping that it was he who would redeem Yisra'el. Yes, and besides all this, it is now the third day since these things happened. (22) Also, certain women of our company amazed us, having arrived early at the tomb; (23) and when they didn't find his body, they came saying that they had also seen a vision of angels, who said that he was alive. (24) Some of us went to the tomb, and found it just like the women had said, but they didn't see him." (25) He said to them, "Foolish men, and slow of heart to believe in all that the prophets have spoken! (26) Didn't the Messiah have to suffer these things and to enter into his glory?" (27) <u>Beginning from Moshe and from all the prophets, he explained to them in all the Scriptures the things concerning himself.</u> (28) They drew near to the village, where they were going, and he acted like he would go further. (29) They urged him, saying, "Stay with us, for it is almost evening, and the day is almost over." He went in to stay with them. (30) It happened, that when he had sat down at the table with them, he took the bread and gave thanks. Breaking it, he gave to them. (31) <u>Their eyes were opened,</u> and they recognized him, and he vanished out of their sight. (32) They said one to another, "Weren't our hearts burning within us, while he spoke to us along the way, and while <u>he opened the Scriptures to us?"</u>

On the road, Yeshua revealed himself to these two men by opening up, or you could even say, properly interpreting the Tanakh (Old Testament) to them. Yeshua revealed to the two men the prophetic foundation of scripture revealing to them the Messiah. He showed them all the prophetic "warning signs" of the things that were to come. Joseph not only explained the two dreams to Pharaoh, but counseled him on what to do concerning the things coming.

Genesis 41:38 HNV Par`oh said to his servants, "Can we find such a one as this, a man in whom is the Spirit of God?"

Pharaoh testified on Josephs' behalf that the Spirit of God lives in him! I guess we could call Joseph a spirit filled man. By this point in his life Joseph had allowed a lot of things to be worked out of his life. His pride was crushed, ambition gone, he couldn't even live as a free man, he was a servant. While he did operate in authority under Potipher, it was stripped from him in the midst of false accusations.

During the time he was in prison he probably came to terms with the fact that he would live the rest of his life there. He was faced with choices. How would he handle his situation? Maybe he came to the same conclusion that Rabbi Shaul would come to later.

Philippians 4:11-13 HNV Not that I speak in respect to lack, for I have learned in whatever state I am, to be content in it. (12) I know how to be humbled, and I know also how to abound. In everything and in all things I have learned the secret both to be filled and to be hungry, both to abound and to be in need. (13) I can do all things through Messiah, who strengthens me.

Joseph was finished trying to prepare for the fulfillment of his own personal dreams. He had learned what it meant to rely on the Father in every situation. When we submit our lives to the Father we don't belong to us anymore. We belong to Him. As we rely on Him, He will order and lead our steps so that we can grow in the way we are intended to.

Proverbs 19:21 HNV There are many plans in a man's heart, but the LORD's counsel will prevail.

When we are following His plan, we are content. The times when we are discontent are the times when we are not following the plan of YHWH or when we desire to stray from it.

The testimony of Joseph from the mouth of Pharaoh was that the Spirit of God lives in him. He spoke this because of the wisdom and discernment that had been worked into Joseph.

Genesis 41:39 HNV Par`oh said to Yosef, "Because God has shown you all of this, there is none so discreet (discerning) and wise as you. - *(Parenthesis added for clarification)*

The same testimony is for all the children of YHWH who accept Him and walk in His ways.

Deuteronomy 4:5-9 HNV Behold, I have taught you statutes and ordinances, even as the LORD my God commanded me, that you should do so in the midst of the land where you go in to possess it. (6) Keep therefore and do them; for this is your wisdom and your understanding in the sight of the peoples, who shall hear all these statutes, and say, Surely this great nation is a wise and understanding people. (7) For what great nation is there, that has a god so near to them, as the LORD our God is whenever we call on him? (8) What great nation is there, that has statutes and ordinances so righteous as all this law, which I set before you this day? (9) Only take heed to yourself, and keep your soul diligently, lest you forget the things which your eyes saw, and lest they depart from your heart all the days of your life; but make them known to your children and your children's children;

Proverbs 18:15-16 HNV The heart of the discerning gets knowledge. The ear of the wise seeks knowledge. (16) A man's gift makes room for him, and brings him before great men.

Hosea 14:9 HNV Who is wise, that he may understand these things? Who is prudent, that he may know them? For the ways of the LORD are right, and the righteous walk in them; But the rebellious stumble in them.

Joseph allowed the wisdom that comes from the Father to be worked into him by simply following where He leads and continuing to walk in His ways. Even Pharaoh knew Joseph was a Hebrew.

Romans 8:28 HNV We know that all things work together for good for those who love God, to those who are called according to his purpose.

Joseph had learned how to deal with the times of famine in His life. When there is a famine, you must have provision on tap! There are times when we may feel uncertain of where our life is going. Do we have peace in knowing that wherever we may be, we have a loving Father who will impart His Spirit to us and lead us through the uncertainty?

When the time came and Joseph was delivered, he was whisked away at almost breakneck speed. He was cleaned up and presented to the king of the whole land. In that very moment he had a choice to make. Do I continue to rely on YHWH for wisdom and understanding, or do I now put on a "hard sell" to Pharaoh to convince him that I'm the man and he would be foolish to throw me back in prison.

If Joseph had stood in front of Pharaoh in pride, he could have been thrown back in prison, or worse yet, he could have been sentenced to death. If Joseph did not fulfill the purpose that the Father had for him, not only would Egypt have been in trouble, but the whole known world would have suffered. As it did come to pass though, Joseph was put into office and given such great authority that only Pharaoh himself was above him. He was given a new name, Zaphnath-Paneah. There are many translations that have been offered for this name. A couple of these suggestions are; Savior of the world, or, He who discovers (reveals) hidden things.

Amos 3:6-7 HNV Does the shofar alarm sound in a city, without the people being afraid? Does evil happen to a city, and the LORD hasn't done it? (7) Surely the Lord GOD will do nothing, unless he reveals his secret to his servants the prophets.

Joseph, being filled with the Spirit of God, had the wisdom, discernment and foresight that came from God to know how to deal with the coming famine. He knew the famine was coming when everyone around him didn't have a clue. He prepared himself, his household, Pharaoh's household and all of Egypt for what was to come. After seven years of fullness and plenty, it dried up.

Do you think it all dried up overnight? Did they wake up one morning and everything they had was gone? Do you think that as the famine came on that the people started to think "something doesn't seem right"?

The people knew that in seven years there would be a famine. I wonder how many scoffers there were. "One more year until the famine hits" they could say while sitting on their front porch sipping umbrella drinks watching the kids swim in the Nile. It's worth noting that for everything that was declared by YHWH in the earth, there were scoffers. For those scoffers, we can pray the same thing that Moses did regarding entering the promised land.

Deuteronomy 9:26-29 HNV I prayed to the LORD, and said, Lord GOD, don't destroy your people and your inheritance, that you have redeemed through your greatness, that you have brought forth out of Egypt with a mighty hand. (27) Remember your servants, Avraham, Yitzchak, and Ya`akov; don't look to the stubbornness of this people, nor to their wickedness, nor to their sin, (28) lest the land whence you brought us out say, Because the LORD was not able to bring them into the land which he promised to them, and because he hated them, he has brought them out to kill them in the wilderness. (29) Yet they are your people and your inheritance, which you brought out by your great power and by your outstretched arm.

Moses prayed to the Father that He would deliver the people into the promise so that it would silence those who had oppressed them before they were brought out of Egypt. That which He says He will do, he will do!

Numbers 23:19 HNV God is not a man, that he should lie, nor the son of man, that he should repent. Has he said, and will he not do it? Or has he spoken, and will he not make it good?

So now, the famine is fully on the land. We see the provision of YHWH through the picture of Joseph.

Genesis 41:53-57 HNV The seven years of plenty, that were in the land of Egypt, came to an end. (54) The seven years of famine began to come, just as Yosef had said. There was famine in all lands, but in all the land of Egypt there was bread. (55) When all the land of Egypt was famished, the people cried to Par`oh for bread, and Par`oh said to all the Egyptians, "Go to Yosef. What he says to you, do." (56) The famine was over all the surface of the earth. Yosef opened all the store houses, and sold to the Egyptians. The famine was severe in the land of Egypt. (57) All countries came into Egypt, to Yosef, to buy grain, because the famine was severe in all the earth.

All people, everywhere, would come to Pharaoh the king of the world. He directed the people to Joseph because he did not have food to give them, but he knew who did.

What I like about this part of the story is that Joseph opened all the storehouses. He did not just open one. His desire was that none who desired bread should go without it. Often times we may hear the answer to our problem, we just don't want to take the necessary steps to receive it. The result is that we heard it, but we didn't heed it.

Genesis 42:1-3 HNV Now Ya`akov saw that there was grain in Egypt, and Ya`akov said to his sons, "Why do you look at one another?" (2) He said, "Behold, I have heard that there is grain in Egypt. Go down there, and buy for us from there, so that we may live, and not die." (3) Yosef's ten brothers went down to buy grain from Egypt.

We sit around looking at the face of the problem, but we wait for someone else to take action concerning it. We could easily fill in the blanks on the following scenario.

- I see that we need _____, but I did_____, so let someone else do that.
- That's not my job

- We compare ourselves to ourselves
- I did more than them so I don't need to do anything else

2 Corinthians 10:12 HNV For we are not bold to number or compare ourselves with some of those who commend themselves. But they themselves, measuring themselves by themselves, and comparing themselves with themselves, are without understanding.
Amos 7:7-8 HNV Thus he showed me and behold, the Lord stood beside a wall made by a plumb line, with a plumb line in his hand. (8) The LORD said to me, "`Amos, what do you see?" I said, "A plumb line." Then the Lord said, "Behold, I will set a plumb line in the midst of my people Yisra'el. I will not again pass by them any more.

The plumb line that has been put among us is the word of YHWH, in written form as well as the walking, living form of Yeshua our savior and Messiah. The whole world had to come before Joseph to buy grain. They could have gone all over Egypt looking for grain, but they would not have found any.

There was only one way they were going to get what they needed for survival in this time of famine. They needed to humble themselves before the one who had the grain to give, and ask for it (buy it). In the Hebrew language, multiple words can come from one word spelled identically. The only variation would be the vowel markings. These related words help explain a deeper function of the word and sometimes can shed a little more understanding of it. The word used for buy here is;

H7666 שׁבר sha`bar- Denominative from H7668; to *deal in grain: - buy, sell.*

H7668 שׁבר sheber - The same as H7667; *grain (as if broken into kernels): - corn, victuals.*

H7667 שׁבר sheber - a *fracture, figuratively ruin; affliction, breaking, broken, bruise, crashing, destruction, hurt, interpretation, vexation.*

Joseph's brothers had to come before him like broken grain. They had to be humble and bow down before their brother (the savior of the world) whom before they had rejected. Remember the dreams that Joseph had regarding his brothers coming and bowing down to him? Another way to look at this is, they had to come to the Savior of the world to obtain the bread that was broken (bread from heaven).

Luke 24:30-32 HNV It happened, that when he had sat down at the table with them, he took the bread and gave thanks. Breaking it, he gave to them. (31) Their eyes were opened, and they recognized him, and he vanished out of their sight. (32) They said one to another, "Weren't our hearts burning within us, while he spoke to us along the way, and while he opened the Scriptures to us?"

John 6:33-35 HNV For the bread of God is that which comes down out of heaven, and gives life to the world." (34) They said therefore to him, "Lord, always give us this bread." (35) Yeshua said to them, "I am the bread of life. He who comes to me will not be hungry, and he who believes in me will never be thirsty.

John 6:51 HNV I am the living bread which came down out of heaven. If anyone eats of this bread, he will live forever. Yes, the bread which I will give for the life of the world is my flesh."

In order to receive this bread, we must come to it broken ourselves.

Psalms 34:18 HNV The LORD is near to those who have a broken heart, and saves those who have a crushed spirit.

Psalms 51:17 HNV The sacrifices of God are a broken spirit. A broken and contrite heart, O God, you will not despise.

Isaiah 57:15 HNV For thus says the high and lofty One who inhabits eternity, whose name is Holy: I dwell in the high and holy place, with him also who is of a contrite and humble spirit, to revive the spirit of the humble, and to revive the heart of the contrite.

2 Timothy 2:22 HNV Flee from youthful lusts; but pursue righteousness, faith, love, and peace with those who call on the Lord out of a pure heart.

So now the brothers of Joseph return home with food and less one brother. Simeon was kept behind as collateral, so to speak, as proof that his brothers would return with Joseph's younger brother Benjamin. When the food runs out, the brothers need to go back in front of Joseph. The problem is, they can't come before him without Benjamin. Jacob refuses to let Benjamin go with his brothers for fear that he will lose him just as he lost Joseph. Jacob relents and allows Benjamin to go because Judah laid his own life on the line if he doesn't return Benjamin safely.

Genesis 43:16-17 HNV When Yosef saw Binyamin with them, he said to the steward of his house, "Bring the men into the house, and butcher an animal, and make ready; for the men will dine with me at noon." (17) The man did as Yosef commanded, and the man brought the men to Yosef's house.

This story takes on new meaning when you look at the whole picture along with the meaning of their names. Joseph now has an Egyptian name that means savior of the world. All the brothers come to the savior of the world on his terms, his way and they could only come to him by Benjamin. The name Benjamin in Hebrew means;

H1144

בִּנְיָמִין

binyâmîyn

bin-yaw-mene'

From H1121 and H3225; *son of* (the) *right hand*; *Binjamin*, youngest son of Jacob; also the tribe descended from him, and its territory: - Benjamin.

The right hand was considered the hand of blessing and strength. So he could just as well have been called son of blessing or son of strength. Are you starting to see a picture and shadow of your relationship with the messiah? You could only come to the Savior, the One who has (and is) the (living) bread, by realizing that it is not in your own strength and merit that you are allowed to come before Him. It's only by the Son of blessing and strength are you able to partake of the bread from Heaven.

How will we be greeted when we see Him? Will he treat us like Joseph did and order a feast prepared for us to dine with Him? How did Yeshua treat his talmidim (disciples) when He saw them after the resurrection but before the ascension?

John 21:10-12 HNV Yeshua said to them, "Bring some of the fish which you have just caught." (11) Shim`on Kefa (*Simon Peter*) went up, and drew the net to land, full of great fish, one hundred fifty-three; and even though there were so many, the net wasn't torn. (12) Yeshua said to them, "Come and eat breakfast." None of the talmidim dared inquire of him, "Who are you?" knowing that it was the Lord.

This is a very prophetic picture of when the Master will return for His Children. The statement, "bring the fish you have caught", will be said to us regarding the souls of men.

Mark 1:17 HNV Yeshua said to them, "Come after me, and I will make you into fishers for men."

Following the statement with come and dine with me is a foreshadow of the marriage supper of the Lamb.

Revelation 19:9 HNV He said to me, "Write, 'Blessed are those who are invited to the marriage supper of the Lamb.'" He said to me, "These are true words of God."

Joseph was equipped to handle the famine because the Spirit of God was within him. He received wisdom, discernment and understanding by the Spirit of God. When the world was overrun with famine, there was a place that had bread. The point is that there was only one place they could find it.

Oftentimes, we know within ourselves when we are in error. We just don't want to take the time to change our ways. There are a lot of parallels between scripture and food. The most obvious for modern times is that we want a whole lot of filler and fluff. I want convenience at either a low cost (or no cost) to me and by the way make it the biggest size you've got.

Having been on many diets in my life, I can honestly say I do know how to eat properly and exercise regularly. Knowing how to do something and doing it are two different things. I know I feel better, think clearer and handle stress better, when I right and exercise. When it comes down to what I know is good for me and what tastes good, hmm now I have to think about it. We approach the word with the same mentality. I know there is life for me within it's pages, I would just rather catch the highlights once a week for an hour instead of putting in all the time and effort involved in reading it for myself.

Are we investing in a good solid spiritual meal, or do we want the fast food that will allow us to feel satisfied, but can send us to an early grave?

NOTES

NOTES

Chapter three

WHAT IS YOUR FOOD?

With all this talk concerning famine, it would be a good idea to know what food we will need to have on hand during the famine. The first thing we need to establish is, what is the food and who gets the food? The short answer is, our food is what the Father sends us. Who gets it? All who will come to gather it!

The word is much like the Manna that was given for all to eat. It provided everything one would need for survival. However, it did not appear every morning as loaves of bread fresh from the oven just waiting to be slathered in butter and jam. It had to be gathered and prepared before it could provide nourishment. Let's take this one step at a time and first look at the food that was provided in the wilderness.

Exodus 16:1-4 HNV They took their journey from Elim, and all the congregation of the children of Yisra'el came to the wilderness of Sin, which is between Elim and Sinai, on the fifteenth day of the second month after their departing out of the land of Egypt. (2) The whole congregation of the children of Yisra'el murmured against Moshe and against Aharon in the wilderness; (3) and the children of Yisra'el said to them, "We wish that we had died by the hand of the LORD in the land of Egypt, when we sat by the meat pots, when we ate our fill of bread, for you have brought us out into this wilderness, to kill this whole assembly with hunger." (4) Then said the LORD to Moshe, "Behold, I will rain bread from the sky for you, and the people shall go out and gather a day's portion every day, that I may test them, whether they will walk in my law, (Torah–Hebrew for teaching and instruction) or not.

In this passage, it has been one month since Israel was brought out of Egypt. They made matzah (unleavened bread) and brought that with them when they left Egypt. Now the time has come when there is no more matzah.

How long do you think you can go without food while walking in the desert? Everyone was reminiscing of the good ol' days when they could sit around at dinner parties eating as much as they wanted and having a good time. Oh, by the way, they were slaves! We have an interesting way of looking back at things sometimes.

They were having a difficult and trying time, so they looked back and complained of times when they thought they were better off even though they weren't free. At this very time they needed to look up and forward to their redeemer, who had delivered them. Instead of looking to Him, they looked back.

If we continually look back in our lives, it will be difficult to walk forward. Have you ever walked backwards when you were a child? How much did you bump into things or even fall? Our lives now are no different. Instead of complaining about our current circumstances, let's seek the bread from Heaven that only the Father can send.

The scripture above in verse four states "Here, I will cause bread to rain down from heaven for you." The Hebrew word for bread here is the word "Lechem"

H3899

לחם

lechem

lekh'-em

From H3898; *food* (for man or beast), especially *bread*, or *grain* (for making it): - ([shew-]) bread, X eat, food, fruit, loaf, meat, victuals. See also H1036.

Does the Father say He will rain down bread, or supply the means for making it? The people had to gather the manna and prepare it before they could eat it. He gave Israel the means to have the food they needed. The Father said He would rain down food. He did not say that He would rain down gourmet seven course meals.

He is supplying their needs by giving them what He knows the people need, not what they want. They are hungry and they are out of food. They were pining for the food they had back in Egypt, but they did not get it. What they did get was some quail and food that they had to go gather and make into bread.

When we get in tough situations, the provision we are given does not always line up with the ideas that we have in our head. We may be in financial need and are crying out for the Father to write us a blank check and drop it in our lap, while the Father is providing us not the cash but the means to get the cash. To say it another way, we may have an opportunity to work overtime, pick up an odd job or provide some type service where we could receive compensation, but we don't want to go out and gather it. We do the same today with our spiritual food.

How many Bibles do you have in your home? How many of them do you read on a daily basis? We know that in order to grow spiritually we need to read and pray. It seems more prevalent, in these current days, that we as believers feel we can grow spiritually without the word. "I don't have time to read my Bible" is spoken more and more every day.

We live out our so very busy lives according to all the things that demand our attention. All the while, the Father is placing the word in front of us to grow in, and to eat, if you will. Our spiritual priorities are out of alignment and we need adjustment. I have even met some people who can quote so much scripture that they think they know it all. These people see themselves as so full that they couldn't eat another bite.

Proverbs 27:7 HNV A full soul loathes a honeycomb; but to a hungry soul, every bitter thing is sweet.

If you get a person who has not eaten in a week, he will appreciate and consume almost anything you set in front of him. You could also take a hungry man and tell him where he could find food and he would travel across town to get it. If however, you find a man who has just finished a huge meal with two helpings of dessert, he will not be very likely to accept another meal, even if it was free.

Are you hungry? I mean, really hungry? Hungry enough to open the book we take for granted and eat from it? We have heard the expression "right under our noses". We have the truth sitting right in front of us but we either don't want it, or don't recognize it as truth.

In many ways we are like the newly redeemed nation of Israel. We are constantly seeing what He has done for us, but have a hard time seeing what He is doing right in front of us at the time He is doing it. This is a testing of our character, in order to see if we will heed the teaching and instruction of our Father. We see this by continuing to read on in verse four;

Exodus 16:4 HNV Then said the LORD to Moshe, "Behold, I will rain bread from the sky for you, and the people shall go out and gather a day's portion every day, that I may test them, whether they will walk in my law, (Torah–Hebrew for teaching and instruction) or not. -*(Parenthesis added for clarification)*

The test is this, will we observe the teaching and instruction that the Father is presenting to us? In order to observe an instruction, we need to know what the instruction is. Israel knew the manna was coming but when it came they didn't know what it was or what to do with it.

Exodus 16:14-15 HNV When the dew that lay had gone, behold, on the surface of the wilderness was a small round thing, small as the frost on the ground. (15) When the children of Yisra'el saw it, they said one to another, (Man hu- מַן־הוּא) "What is it?" For they didn't know what it was. Moshe said to them, "It is the bread which the LORD has given you to eat."

When the people saw the provision of the Father they asked the question, "What is it?" What we call manna is actually two Hebrew words. According to the scripture, the people said "Man Hu" because they didn't know what it was. The first word "mah" or "man" means what. The second word "hu" means he or it. This reveals to us a lot concerning how we should approach new things being revealed to us.

The people of Israel were told that in the morning they would have food from Heaven. When they woke up and saw it, they did not recognize it. Since they did not recognize it, they didn't know what to do with it. They had to be reminded of what had already been said, "this is the bread you were already told about."

Have you ever gone to a new restaurant and tried new foods? How do you respond when the waiter sets something in front of you that you don't recognize? We respond like a child, contemplating if what is before us is even edible. Unfortunately, we treat the word of YHWH the same way at times. When we are presented with something we have not seen before, it may confuse our doctrine so we refuse to accept it and call it "foreign" or inedible.

Hosea 8:11-13 HNV Because Efrayim *(one of the twelve tribes of Isarael)* has multiplied altars for sinning, they became for him altars for sinning. (12) I wrote for him the many things of my law; but they were regarded as a strange (*foreign*) thing. (13) As for the sacrifices of my offerings, they sacrifice flesh and eat it; But the LORD doesn't accept them. Now he will remember their iniquity, and punish their sins. They will return to Egypt.
(Parenthesis added for clarification)

Wow! Can you picture this? The people are given instructions by the Father and are taught how to apply those instructions. Somewhere in the process, the instructions, or the teaching of them, is called foreign or strange, or even profane. The Strong's concordance defines this word as:

H2114

זוּר

zûr

zoor

A primitive root; to *turn* aside (especially for lodging); hence to *be a foreigner, strange, profane*; specifically (active participle) to *commit adultery:* - (come from) another (man, place), fanner, go away, (e-) strange (-r, thing, woman).

Can you imagine taking the very word, teaching and instruction from YHWH and daring to call it foreign, or profane saying it has gone away? In these days we are in, that very thing has happened!

Romans 1:28 HNV Even as they refused to have God in their knowledge, God gave them up to a reprobate mind, to do those things which are not fitting;

Isaiah 5:20-21 HNV Woe to those who call evil good, and good evil; who put darkness for light, and light for darkness; who put bitter for sweet, and sweet for bitter! (21) Woe to those who are wise in their own eyes, and prudent in their own sight!

1 Timothy 4:1 KJV Now the Spirit speaketh expressly, that in the latter times some shall depart from the faith, giving heed to seducing spirits, and doctrines of devils;

2 Timothy 4:2-5 HNV preach the word; be urgent in season and out of season; reprove, rebuke, and exhort, with all patience and teaching. (3) For the time will come when they will not listen to the sound doctrine, but, having itching ears, will heap up for themselves teachers after their own lusts; (4) and will turn away their ears from the truth, and turn aside to fables. (5) But you be sober in all things, suffer hardship, do the work of an evangelist, and fulfill your ministry.

1 Timothy 4:13 HNV Until I come, pay attention to reading, to exhortation, and to teaching.

      The Apostle Paul told Timothy to pay attention to the public reading of scripture. The public reading would be the reading that was taking place in the synagogues every Sabbath. Every week they would read from the Torah, the Prophets and the writings. We know this by the name "old covenant", they knew this by "Tanakh". The Hebrew word "Tanakh" is an acronym, it stands for Torah- the first five books, Nevi'im- the prophets and Ketuvim- the writings, which would be the Psalms, Proverbs and historical books.

2 Timothy 3:12-17 HNV Yes, and all who desire to live godly in Messiah Yeshua will suffer persecution. (13) But evil men and impostors will grow worse and worse, deceiving and being deceived. (14) But you remain in the things which you have learned and have been assured of, knowing from whom you have learned them. (15) From infancy, you have known the sacred writings which are able to make you wise for salvation through faith, which is in Messiah Yeshua. (16) Every writing inspired by God is profitable for teaching, for reproof, for correction, and for instruction which is in righteousness, (17) that the man of God may be complete, thoroughly equipped for every good work.

In this account Rabbi Shaul (the Apostle Paul) tells Timothy to continue in what he has learned and to remember how he was taught the Scripture from the time he was a child. Scripture referred to here, would be the Tanakh. The New Testament did not exist, in print, at this point in time. He goes on to say in verse sixteen that all Scripture is given by the breath (or Spirit) of God, and that all scripture is valuable.
      We see from this account that the Scripture they already had in place, is good to use to teach the truth, to convict a person of sin in their life, to correct faults one may have and to train people how to live rightly. So, by doing all of this it will equip the people for every good work.

      We must be careful that we do not misapply the word that we have been given. It was emphasized that <u>All</u>

Scripture is good and God-breathed and we should keep it in front of us for instruction on how to walk out our daily lives. If we are reading the word properly, it all reveals our Messiah and the heart of the Father. Yeshua (Jesus) told the people that if they were reading their Bibles, you know, the Torah scrolls, properly that they would be able to understand the concept that He really is the Messiah.

John 5:46-47 CJB For if you really believed Moshe, you would believe me; because it was about me that he wrote. (47) But if you don't believe what he wrote, how are you going to believe what I say?"

What an incredible statement! Yeshua was telling the people that if they really and honestly believed what Moses wrote, the Torah, they would believe Yeshua himself because Moses wrote about Him all through the Torah. He then goes on to say that if you don't believe what Moses wrote, you wouldn't believe what Yeshua has to say. We need to understand the complexity of this seemingly simple statement.

If what Yeshua said is true, that we must believe what Moses wrote in order to see Him properly, that raises another question. Do we believe that the Torah Moses wrote is true? How can we say that the Torah is not true and applicable to us today when Yeshua said that in order to recognize Him, you had to believe it? The people He was talking to were the hard-hearted religious teachers.

Do we see the entire Scripture from Genesis to Revelation as being relevant to us? Or are we approaching the word with questions that we already have answered in our minds so that when we find something that we don't agree with we say "that is not good food! Why, it's so old that it's inedible"? If we don't receive the word, our hearts and minds will become hardened and then we will miss the truth that is right in front of us. Paul addresses this to the Corinthian assembly.

2 Corinthians 3:14-18 HNV But their minds were hardened, for until this very day at the reading of the old covenant _the same veil remains_, because _in Messiah it_ **(the veil)** _passes_

away. (15) But to this day, when Moshe is read, *a veil lies on their heart*. (16) But whenever one turns to the Lord, *the veil is taken away*. (17) Now the Lord is the Spirit and where the Spirit of the Lord is, there is liberty. (18) But we all, with *unveiled face* beholding as in a mirror the glory of the Lord, are transformed into the same image from glory to glory, even as from the Lord, the Spirit. -*(italics added for clarification)*

What Paul is saying is that when we come to believe and have faith in the Messiah, the veil to see the word properly is taken away. Notice, nowhere in here does it say that any part of Scripture was taken away from you or that coming to Messiah separated you from any Scripture. The *veil* in order to see was removed!

He goes on to say that in all this you have the Spirit that gives freedom and liberty! When the veil is gone, we can walk in the liberty that only He can give! When we are walking in His spirit, we can see the word properly. As a result of seeing properly, we will become more like Him!

When we come to have faith and believe that Yeshua is the Savior and Messiah for the world, we will have no problem reconciling the "old" and "new" Testaments. We will see them all as One Testament wherein YHWH, through the working of many covenants and promises, reveals not only Himself but His redemption for His people! Let us never forget that the word of YHWH is what we need and must have in order to live the way He desires for us. The word that we have was not given to us around 0-1 AD. It was at the very beginning!

John 1:1-5 HNV In the beginning was the Word, and the Word was with God, and the Word was God. (2) The same was in the beginning with God. (3) All things were made through him. Without him was not anything made that has been made. (4) In him was life, and the life was the light of men. (5) The light shines in the darkness, and the darkness hasn't overcome it.

John 1:9-14 HNV The true light that enlightens everyone was coming into the world. (10) He was in the world, and the world was made through him, and the world didn't recognize him. (11) He came to his own, and those who were his own didn't receive him. (12) But as many as received him, to them he gave the right to become God's children, to those who believe in his name: (13) who were born not of blood, nor of the will of the flesh, nor of the will of man, but of God. (14) The Word became flesh, and lived among us. We saw his glory, such glory as of the one and only Son of the Father, full of grace and truth.

We see the testimony of Scripture here, on behalf of Yeshua, that the very Word of YHWH was in the very beginning! When Yeshua stepped His foot on the earth as a man, He did not become any less the Word of YHWH! I don't think any of us would say that Yeshua our Savior and Messiah was schizophrenic or had a multiple personality disorder. He did not at any point cease being the Word, nor did He at any point change who He is!

Malachi 3:6 HNV "For I, the LORD, don't change; therefore you, sons of Ya`akov, (Jacob/Israel) are not consumed. - *(Parenthesis added for clarification)*

Hebrews 13:8 HNV Yeshua the Messiah is the same yesterday, today, and forever.

  Our Savior not only is the living word who was at the very beginning and doesn't change, but He is also completely and totally one with the Father.

John 1:18 HNV No one has seen God at any time. The one and only Son, who is in the bosom of the Father, he has declared him.

John 10:30 HNV I and the Father are one."

Remember to preface the following scripture with the declaration that Yeshua made here that He and the Father are one.

John 14:21 HNV One who has my mitzvot,
- and keeps them,
- that person is one who loves me.
- One who loves me will be loved by my Father,
- and I will love him,
- and will reveal myself to him."

We were charged by the Savior and Master Himself to Keep His commands. Keeping His commands is how we show Him that we love Him! When we love Him and do what He says, He promised to reveal Himself to us.

John 15:10-14 HNV If you **keep my mitzvot**,

- you will remain in my love;
- even **as I have kept my Father's mitzvot**,
- and remain in his love.
- (11) I have spoken these things to you, that my joy may remain in you, and that your joy may be made full.
- (12) "This is my mitzvah, that you love one another, even as I have loved you.
- (13) Greater love has no one than this, that someone lay down his life for his friends.
- (14) You are my friends,
- if you do whatever I command you.

Yeshua made a declaration here that cannot be overlooked. He makes the statement that **He has kept** the Father's commands! Did the Father's commands contradict what Yeshua came to declare? No! If they did contradict, they would not be counted as being in complete and total unity. They were one in every way!

When Yeshua prayed for his disciples He prayed that we would be one! Not just with the Father, but if we are all one with The Father, and we are all one with Yeshua, then we all would be one with each other! Look at what He prayed in John 17;

John 17:11 HNV I am no more in the world, but these are in the world, and I am coming to you. Holy Father, keep them through your name which you have given me, that they may be one, even as we are.
Yeshua also states that being set apart for holiness comes by the truth. What is truth? Yeshua states "your word is truth"!

John 17:17-21 HNV Sanctify them in your truth. **_Your word is truth_**. (18) As you sent me into the world, even so I have sent them into the world. (19) For their sakes I sanctify myself, that they themselves also may be sanctified in truth. (20) Not for these only do I pray, but for those also who believe in me through their word, (21) that they may all be one; even as you, Father, are in me, and I in you, that they also may be one in us; that the world may believe that you sent me.

The truth is the path we need to walk in! When we stray from the path we are not walking in the full truth that we are intended to walk in.

We were given the word of truth concerning our Messiah and salvation from the beginning. If we agree with the word or not, it does not make it any less the truth. If we are only half obedient, are we really being obedient? Partiality in application of the word of YHWH is still a heart not completely surrendered to the one who redeemed it. The Father addressed this to the people in Malachi.

Malachi 2:5-10 HNV "My covenant was with him of life and shalom; and I gave them to him who he might be reverent toward me; and he was reverent toward me, and stood in awe of my name. (6) The law of truth was in his mouth, and unrighteousness was not found in his lips. He walked with me in shalom and uprightness, and **_turned many away_**

from iniquity. (7) For the Kohen's lips should keep knowledge, and they should seek the law at his mouth; for he is the messenger of the LORD of Armies. (8) But you have turned aside out of the way. You have caused many to stumble in the law. You have corrupted the covenant of Levi," says the LORD of Armies. (9) "Therefore I have also made you contemptible and base before all the people, according to the way **_you have not kept my ways_**, but have had respect for persons in the law. (**_were partial in applying the Torah_**)(10) Don't we all have one father? Hasn't one God created us? Why do we deal treacherously every man against his brother, profaning the covenant of our fathers? - *(Parenthesis added for clarification)*

When Yeshua was led out into the wilderness for forty days, what did He say His sustenance and lifeline was?

Matthew 4:1-4 HNV Then Yeshua was led up by the Spirit into the wilderness to be tempted by the devil. (2) When he had fasted forty days and forty nights, he was hungry afterward. (3) The tempter came and said to him, "If you are the Son of God, command that these stones become bread." (4) But he answered, "It is written, 'Man shall not live by bread alone, but by every word that proceeds out of the mouth of God.'"

When He was tempted, He responded with the word concerning another time that the people of YHWH were tempted and tested.

Deuteronomy 8:1-3 HNV All the mitzvah which I command you this day shall you observe to do, that you may live, and multiply, and go in and possess the land which the LORD swore to your fathers. (2) You shall _remember all the way_ which the LORD your God has led you these forty years in the wilderness, _that he might humble you,_ to prove you, to know what was in your heart, _whether you would keep his mitzvot, or not._ (3) He humbled you, and allowed you to hunger, and fed you with manna, which you didn't know, neither did your fathers know;

- that he might make you know that man does not live by bread only,
- but by _everything_
- that proceeds _out of the mouth of the LORD_ does man live.

Our sustenance, survival and lifeline are dependent upon the word from the Father! Our food is the word from the Father! Yeshua said it was good food and fit for consumption. We will further see what we receive from the mouth of God in the next chapter.

NOTES

NOTES

Chapter Four

RECEIVING FROM THE MOUTH OF GOD

When you speak concerning something you feel especially strong or emotional about, how do you explain or convey how you feel with the ones to whom you are speaking? You would more than likely say that you were "speaking from the heart". What we don't realize is, that this is a biblical concept. Scripturally speaking, *any* time we speak it is from the heart.

Luke 6:45 HNV The good man out of the good treasure of his heart brings out that which is good, and the evil man out of the evil treasure of his heart brings out that which is evil, for out of the abundance of the heart, his mouth speaks.

Who you are, your personality, your thoughts, your ideas and your outlook on life, all come out when you speak to people. All you are is revealed through you as you speak. One thing we forget is it's not always what we say, but how we say it. Have you ever heard someone say something that didn't sound right to you or others around you and they come back with "Oh, I was only joking with you?" If there wasn't some truth to what they said, they wouldn't have said it. Scripture tells us not to behave this way.

Proverbs 26:18-21 HNV Like a madman who shoots firebrands, arrows, and death, (19) is the man who deceives his neighbor and says, "Am I not joking?" (20) For lack of wood a fire goes out. Without gossip, a quarrel dies down. (21) As coals are to hot embers, and wood to fire, so is a contentious man to kindling strife.

Yeshua tells us to pay attention to the words that come out of our mouth.

Matthew 5:37 HNV But let your 'Yes' be 'Yes' and your 'No' be 'No.' hatever is more than these is of the evil one.

Shaul (the Apostle Paul) said something similar to the assembly in Corinth.

2 Corinthians 1:17-19 HNV When I therefore was thus determined, did I show fickleness? Or the things that I purpose, do I purpose according to the flesh, that with me there should be the "Yes, yes" and the "No, no?" (18) But as God is faithful, our word toward you was not "Yes and no." (19) For the Son of God, Yeshua the Messiah, who was preached among you by us, by me, Sila, and Timothy, was not "Yes and no," but in him is "Yes."

James 5:12 HNV But above all things, my brothers, don't swear, neither by heaven, nor by the earth, nor by any other oath; but let your "yes" be "yes," and your "no," "no;" so that you don't fall into hypocrisy.

Shaul is saying something in agreement with what Yeshua had said earlier and it is confirmed by James. Say what you mean and mean what you say. It will all come out anyway. If you are speaking to someone and you don't really believe yourself what you are saying, the one you are speaking to can see through it. If you are speaking things that you shouldn't, it is revealing something concerning your character. One aspect of maturing in our spiritual walk is controlling what we say.

Psalms 39:1 HNV <<For the Chief Musician. For Yedutun. A Psalm by David.>> I said, "I will watch my ways, so that I don't sin with my tongue. I will keep my mouth with a bridle while the wicked is before me."

Notice how David pairs his actions and words together. We need to have our words and actions say the same message. If they conflict, one of them is being deceptive.

Proverbs 10:18-21 HNV He who hides hatred has lying lips. He who utters a slander is a fool. (19) In the multitude of words there is no lack of disobedience, but he who restrains his lips does wisely. (20) The tongue of the righteous is like choice silver. The heart of the wicked is of little worth. (21)

The lips of the righteous feed many, but the foolish die for lack of understanding.

Proverbs 16:1-3 HNV The plans of the heart belong to man, but the answer of the tongue is from the LORD. (2) All the ways of a man are clean in his own eyes; but the LORD weighs the motives. (3) Commit your deeds to the LORD, and your plans shall succeed.

Proverbs 17:27-28 HNV He who spares his words has knowledge. He who is even tempered is a man of understanding. (28) Even a fool, when he keeps silent, is counted wise. When he shuts his lips, he is thought to be discerning.

Zephaniah 3:13 HNV The remnant of Yisra'el will not do iniquity, nor speak lies, neither will a deceitful tongue be found in their mouth, for they will feed and lie down, and no one will make them afraid."

James 1:26 HNV If anyone among you thinks himself to be religious while he doesn't bridle his tongue, but deceives his heart, this man's religion is worthless.

1 Peter 3:8-12 HNV Finally, be all like-minded, compassionate, loving as brothers, tenderhearted, courteous, (9) not rendering evil for evil, or reviling for reviling; but instead blessing; knowing that to this were you called, that you may inherit a blessing. (10) For, "He who would love life, and see good days, let him keep his tongue from evil, and his lips from speaking deceit. (11) Let him turn away from evil, and do good. Let him seek peace, and pursue it. (12) For the eyes of the Lord are on the righteous, and his ears open to their prayer; but the face of the Lord is against those who do evil."

We continue to see a common theme in these scriptures. If we say something, it should be wholeheartedly and backed up with our actions. We have a hard time with controlling our tongue but the Father wants us to be more like Him and His Son. I have yet to find the scripture where the Father looks down on Earth and says it was all a joke. The point is, the Father meant what He said.

Look at some of the things people received from the Father. What did He say? He was either giving instruction in how to live our lives, revealing to us what love is and how to walk in it, or, He was calling people back to Him. He called them back to walk in His word, along with warnings of things that would happen if we choose to continue in our way of life with our backs to Him and are not concerned with what He wants for us.

2 Corinthians 1:17-19 HNV When I therefore was thus determined, did I show fickleness? Or the things that I purpose, do I purpose according to the flesh, that with me there should be the "Yes, yes" and the "No, no?" (18) But as God is faithful, our word toward you was not "Yes and no." (19) For the Son of God, Yeshua the Messiah, who was preached among you by us, by me, Sila, and Timothy, was not "Yes and no," but in him is "Yes."

Jeremiah 6:16 HNV Thus says the LORD, Stand you in the ways and see, and ask for the old paths, where is the good way; and walk therein, and you shall find rest for your souls: but they said, We will not walk [therein].

This verse of scripture reveals something to us. We want a newer, bigger, better, fresher and faster way of doing things. We in America are a spoiled society who want what we want, when we want it and if we don't get it fast enough, we want to speak to the Manager. The verse says that in order to find rest, we must return to the ancient paths, the paths of our forefathers, who had no choice but to walk by faith.

Do you feel that at times you need rest? Do you struggle with fear and worry? If you had a sickness and were presented with the cure, would you take it? We live in spiritual unrest and need rest, but when presented with the antidote we need, we respond to it being presented to us as if it were a slap in the face. Almost like we are saying "how dare you say I need anything from anyone!"

If we were in a desert, would we take water? If we are spiritually thirsty and in need of water to refresh us, why do we not accept it? Is the cost too high? The cost has already been paid! We just need to take it and walk with it. Yeshua deals with this attitude in the book of Revelation in the letter to the church of Laodicea.

Revelation 3:15-19 HNV "I know your works, that you are neither cold nor hot. I wish you were cold or hot. (16) So, because you are lukewarm, and neither hot nor cold, I will vomit you out of my mouth. (17) Because you say, 'I am rich, and have gotten riches, and have need of nothing;' and don't know that you are the wretched one, miserable, poor, blind, and naked; (18) I counsel you to buy from me gold refined by fire, that you may become rich; and white garments, that you may clothe yourself, and that the shame of your nakedness may not be revealed; and eye salve to anoint your eyes, that you may see. (19) As many as I love, I reprove and chasten. Be zealous therefore, and repent.

I am hearing the prayers that are being offered up to the throne by the people of God. There is no doubt that we need Him. There is no doubt that we are asking, some with great tears and intercession, for YHWH to intervene in our lives and in the lives of our brothers and sisters.

I often hear a desperate plea to send us a fresh word from Heaven. I have even heard of people crying out for the Father to send people like the prophets of old to help direct them or others. My heart is burdened. We cry out for an answer and when it comes we don't accept it as the answer. We want YHWH to show Himself strong in the Earth, especially in our situations, but we tell Him how He is to do it.

How much new word and Revelation of the Spirit of YHWH will you receive when you are ignoring what He is telling you? We are no different today than in Jeremiah's day. Let's continue reading in chapter six starting in verse sixteen.

Jeremiah 6:16-19 CJB Here is what Adonai says:

- "Stand at the crossroads and look; ask about the ancient paths, 'Which one is the good way?'
- Take it, and you will find rest for your souls.
- But they said, 'We will not take it.'
- (17) I appointed sentinels to direct them: 'Listen for the sound of the shofar.'
- But they said, 'We will not listen.'
- (18) So hear, you nations; know, you assembly, what there is against them. (19) Hear, oh earth!
- I am going to bring disaster on this people;
- **_it is the consequence of their own way of thinking;_**
- for they pay no attention to my words;
- and as for my Torah,
- they reject it.

We are a generation today that wants supernatural intervention in our lives. We don't however, want the foundation of the word that we need in order to learn how to walk free. We think that because something supernatural has happened, or because we have seen some sign or wonder that God is in our midst. Do we seek signs or do we seek the Father? We don't want the word of YHWH, we want a horse and pony show.

Yeshua gave us a parable that addresses this mindset. It is addressed in the parable of the rich man and Lazarus the beggar.

Luke 16:19-31 HNV "Now there was a certain rich man, and he was clothed in purple and fine linen, living in luxury every day. (20) A certain beggar, named El'azar, was laid at his gate, full of sores, (21) and desiring to be fed with the crumbs that fell from the rich man's table. Yes, even the dogs came and licked his sores. (22) It happened that the beggar died, and that he was carried away by the angels to Avraham's bosom. The rich man also died, and was buried. (23) In She'ol, he lifted up his eyes, being in torment, and saw Avraham far off, and El'azar at his bosom. (24) He cried and said, 'Father Avraham, have mercy on me, and send El'azar, that he may dip the tip of his finger in water, and cool my tongue! For I am in anguish in this flame.' (25) "But Avraham said, 'Son, remember that you, in your lifetime, received your good things, and El'azar, in like manner, bad things. But now here he is comforted and you are in anguish. (26) Besides all this, between us and you there is a great gulf fixed, that those who want to pass from here to you are not able, and that none may cross over from there to us.'

Do you think that the rich man, who had no need of anything from anyone, was too prideful to ask for help now that he is seeing the consequences of his actions? He knows the truth of the word now. Now he understands that the wages of sin is death.

His sin was not that he had money. His sin was he had no compassion on his brother. He was not concerned with anyone else's life or what anyone else had to say, even God.

Now that he knows the truth, he asks for some miraculous sign to warn his family. Still thinking of himself, his brothers, what about his neighbors? Did he care enough about the welfare of his neighbors to ask for someone to be sent to them?

(27) "He said, 'I ask you therefore, father, that you would send him to my father's house; (28) for I have five brothers, that he may testify to them, so they won't also come into this place of torment.'

What do you think the response is to the rich man? Was he told "hey, that's a great idea, if the people see a sign they will receive!"? Did Yeshua tell the accuser when tempted that man shall not live by bread alone but by every sign and wonder that comes from God? NO! The response that was given in the parable that Yeshua was telling was to be obedient to the word of YHWH.

(29) "But Avraham said to him,
- 'They have Moshe (Torah)
- and the prophets. (calling all to return to the Father and His word)
- Let them listen to them.' (Shama- be obedient to)
- (30) "He said, 'No, father Avraham, but if one goes to them from the dead, they will repent.'

Listen to what the rich man is saying, "No, no, no that won't work, they won't listen to that, they need a sign!"

- (31) "He said to him,
- 'If they don't listen to Moshe
- and the prophets,
- neither will they be persuaded
- ***if one rises from the dead.***'"

This parable tells us a lot. Verse thirty-one reiterates what Yeshua had said before, that if we are unwilling to accept what Moses said, we won't be willing to receive who He is and what He says! He says in this verse that if a person will not receive from the Torah and the Prophets, they won't believe in Him, even if He was to be raised from the dead! We all know the story, he was raised from the dead! So, how many people receive Jesus as Lord, say the sinners prayer and never read their Bible, or go to a congregation or assembly, or pray with the purpose of only spending time with the Father?

I have even heard people say that they don't want the Father, they want the Son. What a misconception of truth! Yeshua, who is the word made flesh, was the means to get to the Father! Our goal is to be in communion with the Father! We accomplish that by being in communion and unity with Yeshua because He and the Father are one! We walk in union with the Messiah by learning from the word (which is Yeshua- the word made flesh) the ways in which we should walk. The word of YHWH will point us in the direction of Messiah Yeshua if we are reading it properly.

Romans 10:4 CJB For the goal at which the Torah aims is the Messiah, who offers righteousness to everyone who trusts.

In the story above, the rich man asked for someone to be sent to his family. He was told that they have been sent the word and the prophets, listen to them. We often like words from the prophets in scripture. They are full of mystery, depth of questions and splendor. We may even like trying to figure out some of the prophecies. They are like riddles to us.

There is not one thing wrong with diving into the word of YHWH. Where we get in trouble is when we mishandle or misinterpret it. We view the words of the prophets as a great word from God, when it's convenient. If it is a strong word of prosperity it's for us all the way. If it is a strong word of rebuke, it has got to be for someone else. As for the prophets, the Father said he will speak to them.

Amos 3:7 HNV Surely the Lord GOD will do nothing, unless he reveals his secret to his servants the prophets.

We're hearing a lot in this time about sending prophets to bring the word. I feel we are not going to get much more "new spiritual revelation" until we learn to be obedient to the words the prophets have already spoken. We need to repent for our hearts not searching out the Fathers will, and for not searching the word we already have.

The Father will speak the word to His people. He will never contradict what He has already said. When the prophets come and bring the word with them, what word is it? It is the word of the LORD!

If a prophet were to come to us and try to entice us into idolatry, we would run away from them. If they would come to us and tell us to throw our Bibles away, we would stay away from them. Sometimes it's not that transparent.

What do we do when we are told that part of the word is insignificant? How do you respond to a person that would tell you the word is not for you, but for someone else? That person will lead us away from the path we are supposed to walk in.

Deuteronomy 13:1-5 (CJB) "If a prophet or someone who gets messages while dreaming arises among you and he gives you a sign or wonder, (2) and the sign or wonder comes about as he predicted when he said, 'Let's follow other gods, which you have not known; and let us serve them,' (3) you are not to listen to what that prophet or dreamer says. For Adonai your God is testing you, in order to find out whether you really do love Adonai your God with all your heart and being. (4) You are to follow Adonai your God, fear him, obey his mitzvot, listen to what he says, serve him and cling to him; (5) and that prophet or dreamer is to be put to death; because he urged rebellion against Adonai your God, who brought you out of the land of Egypt and redeemed you from a life of slavery; in order to seduce you away from the path Adonai your God ordered you to follow. This is how you are to rid your community of this wickedness.

This portion of scripture was used as a test to see if a prophet really was a prophet of YHWH. This also was given for us to see if we loved YHWH or not. We are warned that people will come into our lives and say that they are from God. Then, they will try to lead us off the true path we are to walk in.

Do we follow the word we have been given? Or, do we follow a smooth talker who is really good at twisting the word to make us think that some part of it is outdated and inapplicable? If they could, they would reason away the word using a perverse humanistic mindset or new age philosophy.

We are to follow the word of the LORD and walk in the way that was given to us. We are not to walk in the ways of the world. We are to walk according to the ways and promises of our Father, and flee anything or anyone that would lead us astray.

After wandering in the wilderness for forty years, it was time for Israel to enter into the land that was promised. The problem was, there were people in the land that needed expelled from it. They had to walk in faith that if they started to move into the land, the Father would go before them. They moved and He did.

Now that they were in the land, was their faith walk over? They had to continue to walk in faith once they were in the promise. They were told that people would rise up among them, some would be good, some would not. They were warned to follow only the one who would rise up that had the word from the Father in his mouth.

Deuteronomy 18:9-15 HNV When you are come into the land which the LORD your God gives you, you shall not learn to do after the abominations of those nations. (10) There shall not be found with you anyone who makes his son or his daughter to pass through the fire, one who uses divination, one who practices sorcery, or an enchanter, or a sorcerer, (11) or a charmer, or a consulter with a familiar spirit, or a wizard, or a necromancer. (12) For whoever does these things is an abomination to the LORD: and because of these abominations the LORD your God does drive them out from before you. (13) You shall be perfect with the LORD your God. (14) For these nations, that you shall dispossess, listen to those who practice sorcery, and to diviners; but as for you, the LORD your God has not allowed you so to do. (15) The LORD your God will raise up to you a prophet from the midst of you, of your brothers, like me; to him you shall listen;

These scriptures say that a prophet will be raised up from among their own kinsmen and to listen to him. We know that many prophets were raised up. How would the people be able to know and discern of whom this prophecy is speaking? Read a little further for the answer.

Deuteronomy 18:18-19 HNV I will raise them up a prophet from
- among their brothers, like you;
- and I will put **my words** in his mouth,
- and he shall speak to them
- *all that **I** shall command* him.
- (19) It shall happen, that whoever will not listen (SHAMA)
- to **my words**
- which *he shall speak*
- *in my name*,
- I will require it of him.

This is a Messianic Prophecy! This is speaking of Yeshua our Messiah! It tells us that we will know to follow Him, because He speaks the words of the Father. He will be raised up from among the people, just like Moses was.

If He did not speak the words of the Father, He would not have fulfilled this prophecy. Yeshua said that he did nothing of His own initiative. He also said that He said nothing of His own initiative. All that He said and did was from the Father. They are one!

John 5:43 HNV I have come in my Father's name, and you don't receive me. If another comes in his own name, you will receive him.

John 6:44-45 HNV No one can come to me unless the Father who sent me draws him, and I will raise him up in the last day. (45) It is written in the prophets, 'They will all be taught by God.' Therefore everyone who hears from the Father, and has learned, comes to me.

John 6:63 HNV It is the spirit who gives life. The flesh profits nothing. The words that I speak to you are spirit, and are life.

John 14:10 HNV Don't you believe that I am in the Father, and the Father in me? The words that I tell you, I speak not from myself; but the Father who lives in me does his works.

John 17:6-17 HNV I revealed your name to the people whom you have given me out of the world. They were yours, and you have given them to me. ***They have kept your word***. (7) Now they have known that all things whatever you have given me are <u>*from you,*</u> (8) for the <u>words which you have given me</u> <u>I have given to them</u>, and ***they received them***, and knew for sure that I came forth from you, and they have believed that you sent me. (9) I pray for them. I don't pray for the world, but for those whom you have given me, for they are yours. (10) All things that are mine are yours, and yours are mine, and I am glorified in them. (11) I am no more in the world, but these are in the world, and I am coming to you. Holy Father, keep them through your name which you have given me, <u>*that they may be one, even as we are.*</u> (12) While I was with them in the world, I kept them in your name. Those whom you have given me I have kept. None of them is lost, except the son of destruction, that the Scripture might be fulfilled. (13) But now I come to you, and I say these things in the world, that they may have my joy made full in themselves. (14) ***I have given them your word. The world hated them,*** because they are not of the world, even as I am not of the world. (15) I pray not that you would take them from the world, but that you would keep them from the evil one. (16) They are not of the world even as I am not of the world.
- (17) Sanctify them (set them apart)
- in your truth.
- ***Your word is truth.***

We see this prayer in the lives of believers today. Verse fourteen says that Yeshua gave his disciples the word of the Father and as a result, the world hated them.

When you have the word inside of you, the world doesn't like you much. You were made to live in the world. You were made to live in communion with the One who created you. You were given the word and as a result, you were set apart for holiness.

We see that you were set apart by the truth, and the truth is the word. The more of the word you receive in your life, the more you will notice the world moving away from you. The world does not want to be sanctified by the word of YHWH. We as believers should readily receive being sanctified and set apart for our God. Yeshua also says that the word which He has spoken is what we will be judged by on the last day.

John 12:48-50 HNV He who rejects me, and doesn't receive my sayings, has one who judges him. The word that I spoke, the same will judge him in the last day. (49) For I spoke not from myself, but the Father who sent me, he gave me a mitzvah, <u>what I should say</u>, and <u>what I should speak</u>. (50) I know that his mitzvah is eternal life. The things therefore which I speak, even **as the Father has said to me, so I speak.**"

What do we receive by the mouth of God? I know it sounds so simple, but we don't think about it. Today, do we receive from the mouth of God or the Spirit of God? Do you literally hear His voice every day or were you supposed to follow the word, directed by the Spirit?

This was one problem that was brought up in accusation against Moses by Aaron and Miriam. The thought was "we hear from God too". If the Father really was speaking to everyone who says they hear Him, as much as they say they hear Him, one would have to say that God is Schizophrenic and can't make up His mind. The truth is, Aaron and Miriam did hear from the Father. However, no one conversed with the Father like Moses did. By listening to some people you would think that the Father spoke with them more than Abraham, Isaac, Jacob and Moses combined.

Numbers 12:1-8 HNV Miryam and Aharon spoke against Moshe because of the Kushite woman whom he had married; for he had married a Kushite woman. (2) They said, Has the LORD indeed spoken only with Moshe? Hasn't he spoken also with us? the LORD heard it. (3) Now the man Moshe was very humble, above all the men who were on the surface of the earth. (4) The LORD spoke suddenly to Moshe, and to Aharon, and to Miryam, Come out you three to the tent of meeting. They three came out. (5) The LORD came down in a pillar of cloud, and stood at the door of the Tent, and called Aharon and Miryam; and they both came forth. (6) He said, Hear now my words:
- if there be a prophet among you,
- I the LORD will make myself known to him in a vision,
- I will speak with him in a dream.
- (7) My servant Moshe is not so; he is faithful in all my house:
- (8) *with him will I speak mouth to mouth,*
- even manifestly,
- and not in dark speeches; (riddles)
- and the form of the LORD shall he see:
- why then were you not afraid to speak against my servant, against Moshe?

How awesome, to have the testimony of speaking face to face with the creator of the universe! Furthermore, he wrote down all the things that were told to him! Are we willing to follow it? Yeshua said that if we believed Moses, we would believe Him!

John 5:46-47 CJB For if you really believed Moshe, you would believe me; because it was about me that he wrote. (47) But if you don't believe what he wrote, how are you going to believe what I say?"

Yeshua said that if we are properly reading what was written, we would see Him all through it! We need to take the veil off that lies over our heart toward the restoration of the ways of the Father and walk the way that He said to walk.

We often hear the account of the Father speaking with Moses as face to face. It's not like that with anyone else! But it still goes deeper! Face to face would be paniym v' paniym. This is not what it says in the text. In the Hebrew it would be Peh el Peh, mouth to mouth! The Father placed His words in Moses' mouth and in turn Moses spoke it to the people. The Father spoke and breathed the word and Spirit (breath that accompanies words) of Himself into the breath and spirit of Moshe, who in turn imparted it to the people!

Exodus 4:15-16 HNV You (Moses) shall speak to him (Aaron), and put the words in his mouth. I will be with your mouth, and with his mouth, and will teach you what you shall do. (16) He will be your spokesman to the people; and it will happen, that he will be to you a mouth, and you will be to him as God.

Isaiah 51:16 HNV I have put my words in your mouth, and have covered you in the shadow of my hand, that I may plant the heavens, and lay the foundations of the earth, and tell Tziyon, You are my people.

Isaiah 59:20-21 HNV A Redeemer will come to Tziyon, and to those who turn from disobedience in Ya`akov, says the LORD. (21) As for me, this is my covenant with them, says the LORD: my Spirit who is on you, and my words which I have put in your mouth, shall not depart out of your mouth, nor out of the mouth of your seed, nor out of the mouth of your seed's seed, says the LORD, from henceforth and forever.

Jeremiah 1:9 HNV Then the LORD put forth his hand, and touched my mouth; and the LORD said to me, Behold, I have put my words in your mouth:

Jeremiah 5:14 HNV Therefore thus says the LORD, the God Tzeva'ot, Because you speak this word, behold, I will make my words in your mouth fire, and this people wood, and it shall devour them.

The Father placed His words in Moses' mouth. Moses in turn spoke those words to the people and furthermore, he wrote them down. Do we want life? Then we should recognize that our life, living and sustenance comes directly from the mouth of YHWH.

There is a remnant who truly desires a deeper relationship with the Father. It is not as hard as we make it. The Father Himself encourages us that we can do it! It seems our first step is to turn our hearts to Him and start learning how to walk in His ways. Many want to see what God can do for them, others want to spend time with Him and learn how to be in a relationship with Him. He would not tell us to seek Him and then punish us because we cannot find Him. He is not hiding. He would not give us His word and say it is to teach us the way in which to have life, then tell us that it was a typo.

Psalms 103:7 HNV He made known his _ways_ to Moshe, his _deeds_ to the children of Yisra'el.

Do we want to know about the Father? To look at things that were done on our behalf? Or would we rather be there in His presence communing with Him, walking with Him in His way? Sometimes we try to reason ourselves out of simple obedience to the word. By doing so, we miss out on what was intended for us by the mouth of YHWH.

There is something to be said about knowing and walking in obedience to the way of YHWH. Think of your children. If you told them to go sit on the porch swing and they go sit on the bench, were they obedient? One might say, well at least they're sitting down and that is what's important.

We reason within ourselves that if we don't fully comprehend the "why" or the reason behind what we are being asked to do, we don't need to do it. The child, in the narrative above, goes out on the porch and sits on the bench, only to discover that it was just painted. Now, the clothes that were just purchased for the child are ruined and the child is in need of new clothing.

Do you need to know the why behind something in order to be obedient to it? You can ask anyone who has served in the armed forces if that would work. Imagine that you are in the heat of battle and your sergeant tells you to jump in the foxhole. You turn around and say to him that you don't understand why you need to do that right now this very second. You continue that you feel your sergeant is just being a little too gung-ho in his observance of military training. You could go on and on but you are cut short by the bomb that went off that you didn't know anything about. If you had only listened to the word you were given, without trying to reason your way out of it, you would be alive.

When we see things in the word that we don't agree with, who's wrong?

NOTES

NOTES

Chapter Five

Is the word burdensome?

2 Timothy 3:16-17 HNV Every writing inspired by God is profitable for teaching, for reproof, for correction, and for instruction which is in righteousness, (17) that the man of God may be complete, thoroughly equipped for every good work.

2 Peter 1:20-21 HNV knowing this first, that no prophecy of Scripture is of private interpretation. (21) For no prophecy ever came by the will of man: but holy men of God spoke, being moved by the Holy Spirit.

Even in prophecy, we must let the word be the guide for the interpretation of that prophecy. All scripture must stay in harmony in order to be called the word of God. In the above scripture reference, what scripture do you think Shaul is speaking of to Timothy? At this time, the New Testament had not been compiled and canonized as scripture. Wherever you see "scripture" or "word" in the New Testament, they are talking about the "Old Testament".

We only view this as a problem because we have been taught that we don't need it or that it was for another time, even a different people. The whole word of YHWH is applicable to us all today. Jew or Gentile is not the question. The word is for those naturally born Jewish, and all those who are grafted in to the promises and covenant. As believers, we are grafted into His promises and covenant.

Numbers 15:28-29 HNV The Kohen shall make atonement for the soul who errs, when he sins unwittingly, before the LORD, to make atonement for him; and he shall be forgiven. (29) You shall have one law for him who does anything unwittingly, for him who is native-born among the children of Yisra'el, and for the stranger who lives as a foreigner among them.

Exodus 12:49 HNV One law (Torah, teaching) shall be to him who is born at home, and to the stranger who lives as a foreigner among you."

Leviticus 24:22 KJV Ye shall have one manner of law, as well for the stranger, as for one of your own country: for I [am] the LORD your God.

Numbers 15:16 HNV One law (Torah, teaching) and one ordinance shall be for you, and for the stranger who lives as a foreigner with you.

Deuteronomy 30:10-14 HNV if you shall obey the voice of the LORD your God, to keep his mitzvot and his statutes which are written in this scroll of the Torah; if you turn to the LORD your God with all your heart, and with all your soul. (11) For this mitzvah which I command you this day, **_it is not too hard for you_**, **_neither is it far off_**. (12) It is not in heaven, that you should say, Who shall go up for us to heaven, and bring it to us, and make us to hear it, that we may do it? (13) Neither is it beyond the sea, that you should say, Who shall go over the sea for us, and bring it to us, and make us to hear it, that we may do it?
- (14) But the word is very near to you,
- in your mouth,
- and in your heart,
- **_that you may do it_**.

When the father speaks we need to listen. Remember, out of the mouth comes what is in the heart. Notice the connection in verse fourteen above: it is in your mouth, because it is in your heart. What we say is a reflection of who we are.

Matthew 12:34 HNV You offspring of vipers, how can you, being evil, speak good things? For out of the abundance of the heart, the mouth speaks.

If we are to watch what comes from _our_ mouth, how much more should we pay attention to what came from the mouth of YHWH!

Matthew 4:4 HNV But he answered, "It is written, 'Man shall not live by bread alone, but by every word that proceeds out of the mouth of God.'"

Deuteronomy 8:2-3 HNV You shall remember all the way which the LORD your God has led you these forty years in the wilderness, that he might humble you, to prove you, to know what was in your heart, whether you would keep his mitzvot, or not. (3) He humbled you, and allowed you to hunger, and fed you with manna, which you didn't know, neither did your fathers know; that he might make you know that man does not live by bread only, **_but by everything that proceeds out of the mouth of the LORD does man live_**.

King David makes the connection between the word and the heart. He also connects that with an uplifted spirit. He said that he delights in the word of YHWH.

Psalms 119:9-16 HNV How can a young man keep his way pure? By living according to your word. (10) With my whole heart, I have sought you. Don't let me wander from your mitzvot. (11) I have hidden your word in my heart, that I might not sin against you. (12) Blessed are you, LORD. Teach me your statutes. (13) With my lips, I have declared all the ordinances of your mouth. (14) I have rejoiced in the way of your testimonies, as much as in all riches. (15) I will meditate on your precepts, and consider your ways. (16) I will delight myself in your statutes. I will not forget your word.

King David starts this stanza in Psalm 119 by asking a question that many today ask. How can we keep our way (path) pure? He answers, we must guard our hearts in the ways of the word! Walking in the word of YHWH is not a burden, it is our delight.

We seek the Father with all our heart and in seeking Him, we will not stray from His commands. The living, breathing word of the LORD is what we will put in our heart. The result is that we won't desire to sin. We will then do as

David did, he blesses the LORD and asks for the Father to teach him his laws, so that he can proclaim all the rulings that were spoken.

King David closes with stating that he will meditate on the things that were declared and will keep his eyes on the path that they should be. He will find delight in and will not forget the word. The word is not a burden for the believer, it is His delight!

Psalms 1:1-6 HNV Blessed is the man who doesn't walk in the counsel of the wicked, nor stand in the way of sinners, nor sit in the seat of scoffers; (2) but **his delight** is in the LORD's law (Torah). On his law he meditates day and night. (3) He will be like a tree planted by the streams of water, that brings forth its fruit in its season, whose leaf also does not wither. Whatever he does shall prosper. (4) The wicked are not so, but are like the chaff which the wind drives away. (5) Therefore the wicked shall not stand in the judgment, nor sinners in the congregation of the righteous. (6) For the LORD knows the way of the righteous, but the way of the wicked shall perish.

Psalms 16:11 HNV You will show me the path of life. In your presence is fullness of joy. In your right hand there are pleasures forevermore.

Psalms 119:89-92 HNV LORD, your word is settled in heaven forever. (90) Your faithfulness is to all generations. You have established the earth, and it remains. (91) Your laws remain to this day, for all things serve you. (92) Unless your law had been my delight, I would have perished in my affliction.

Isaiah 58:13-14 CJB "If you hold back your foot on Shabbat from pursuing your own interests on my holy day; if you call Shabbat a delight, Adonai's holy day, worth honoring; then honor it by not doing your usual things or pursuing your interests or speaking about them. (14) If you do, you will find delight in Adonai -- I will make you ride on the heights of the land and feed you with the heritage of your ancestor Ya`akov, for the mouth of Adonai has spoken."

Psalms 37:1-5 HNV <<By David.>> Don't fret because of evil-doers, neither be envious against those who work unrighteousness. (2) For they shall soon be cut down like the grass, and wither like the green herb. (3) Trust in the LORD, and do good. Dwell in the land, and enjoy safe pasture. (4) Also <u>*delight yourself in the LORD*</u>, and he will give you the desires of your heart. (5) Commit your way to the LORD. Trust also in him, and he will do this:

I love what David wrote in Psalms 37:3 trust in the Lord could also mean, "feed on faithfulness". Feeding on faithfulness comes after trusting and having faith in YHWH. When we feed on faithfulness, we will be delighting ourselves in Him.

When we are hungry, what food are we looking for? When we are hungry we entertain thoughts of what sounds good to us at the time. We turn to the person next to us and say, "Are you hungry? What sounds good to you? How about we go for a pizza or a steak?". So, what are you hungry for?

Even in travelling, you may not know the area very well but when it comes time to eat and you are hungry, you look for something familiar to you. Is it a burden for you to find what you really want? It is not burdensome because it is your desire! You will go out of the way to find what you really want. When you find it you will rejoice in it.

I went to Israel a few years ago with a group of people. If you have not been, you should go. I feel it would change the life of every believer to see and experience all the places you read about. You can even feel the presence of YHWH in a more tangible way. There is no way to explain it other than the fact that He said it belongs to Him. He put His name there.

We saw amazing sights and walked all over the land. Then we walked some more. Did I say that we did a lot of walking? We were enjoying the experience, but we weren't accustomed to the physical exertion. Even the children (teens) were exhausted.

During this time there was one lady with us that was a picky eater. She loved the experience of being in the land, but the food was unfamiliar to her. She did not care much for trying new food. She loved the land, but was very uncomfortable and desired something of the familiar things she was used to. Towards the end, we overheard that there was a McDonalds and a Burger King over on Ben Yehuda Street. It was amazing! All these people who were tired, exhausted, hurting, achy and just wanted to rest, sprung to their feet and took off almost in a run to get to what they wanted. We didn't even know where the street was! We were pointed in the general direction and we were off on the journey!

We assumed that we would figure out how to get there along the way. Talk about the blind leading the blind. A group of people walking around a town that they are unfamiliar with, asking people as they came across them "Do you know the way to our destination?" We did find what we were looking for, and we did get a burger.

After we ate and were satisfied, all these people who had just showed signs of exuberant life, reverted back to their former state. We went back to the hotel and rested the remainder of the evening.

At the time that we were tired and sore, we had sprung to life again. Our spirit was revived when we heard that what we desired could be found not far from here. We were willing to go through a couple more blisters and a little more discomfort to get to the goal of what we desired.

There are two ways to look at this. First, you could say that if you are hungry enough, you will do whatever you need to do to get to the goal. The other way you could look at this is much like Israel did in the wilderness.

Think about it in this aspect; we were in the land of Israel! We were walking in the land that was promised in Scripture. We were walking on the same ground that our Messiah would have walked on. We were seeing the places where He performed miracles. We could stand on the Mount of Olives and read the words that He spoke from this very place. Yet in the midst of it all, there were some with a great desire for the old familiar things that we were accustomed to.

We hold on to traditions and customs of our old nature. We aren't willing to let them go in order to walk in the promise and live life experiencing all the aspects of the promise. We don't want to accept new things that we may have never seen before.

There is so much in the word that we have yet to experience. How much of the word are we missing out on because we are unable or unwilling to recognize that it is food for us. We look at the word as burdensome because we don't know it. We look at something new and immediately declare it unsuitable for us because it makes our selfish desires accountable to change.

We are quick to complain any time we need to change. What about when we do something wrong? How do we respond when we are caught in it? We try to defend our position and convince everyone that we are not in error. You might even say "Can't you see that they are just picking on me?" How about "they are just cramping my style"? When the facts come out, we were wrong. Any person that would now bring correction to us is just being a burden or putting a heavy yoke on us. Correction is not burdensome to receive when your heart is to walk in the way of righteousness.

Leviticus 26:23-26 HNV "'If by these things you won't be reformed to me, but will walk contrary to me; (24) then I will also walk contrary to you; and I will strike you, even I, seven times for your sins. (25) I will bring a sword upon you, that will execute the vengeance of the covenant; and you will be gathered together within your cities: and I will send the pestilence among you; and you will be delivered into the hand of the enemy. (26) When I break your staff of bread, ten women shall bake your bread in one oven, and they shall deliver your bread again by weight: and you shall eat, and not be satisfied.

Proverbs 10:16-17 HNV The labor of the righteous leads to life. The increase of the wicked leads to sin. (17) He is in the way of life who heeds correction, but he who forsakes reproof leads others astray.

Proverbs 12:1 HNV Whoever loves correction loves knowledge, but he who hates reproof is stupid.

Proverbs 15:9-10 HNV The way of the wicked is an abomination to the LORD, but he loves him who follows after righteousness. (10) There is stern discipline for one who forsakes the way: whoever hates reproof shall die.

Proverbs 15:31-33 HNV The ear that listens to reproof lives, and will be at home among the wise. (32) He who refuses correction despises his own soul, but he who listens to reproof gets understanding. (33) The fear of the LORD teaches wisdom. Before honor is humility.

If we are willing to receive correction and discipline we will receive help with the burden. When we are obedient, we will be equipped to walk in the way. When we are doing what we need to do, in order to finish the task before us, we will be given the help to carry any burden we may have. When we are unwilling to receive the help that the Father is trying to give us, we carry the burden ourselves. We all have a task before us. Will we walk in it and receive the help we need in order to complete the task?

Numbers 11:16-17 HNV The LORD said to Moshe, Gather to me seventy men of the elders of Yisra'el, whom you know to be the elders of the people, and officers over them; and bring them to the tent of meeting, that they may stand there with you. (17) I will come down and talk with you there: and I will take of the Spirit which is on you, and will put it on them; and they shall bear the burden of the people with you, that you not bear it yourself alone.

The only way to stay on the path and fulfill the call we have been given, is to walk humbly before our LORD. When we are humble, we receive the empowerment that we need to reach the goal. We understand that we cannot do it alone.

1 Peter 5:5-7 HNV Likewise, you younger ones, be subject to the elder. Yes, all of you gird yourselves with humility, to subject yourselves to one another; for "God resists the proud, but gives grace to the humble." (6) Humble yourselves therefore under the mighty hand of God, that he may exalt you in due time; (7) casting all your worries on him, because he cares for you.

We need to learn how to let it go. Whatever the "it" in your situation is, give it up and cast your anxiety, worry and stress upon Him. He will help you carry the burden.

Matthew 11:28-30 HNV "Come to me, all you who labor and are heavily burdened, and I will give you rest. (29) Take my yoke upon you, and learn from me, for I am gentle and lowly in heart; and you will find rest for your souls. (30) For my yoke is easy, and my burden is light."

How hard is it to listen to the one that you love? When you love someone, you can't wait to spend time with them. You want to hear their voice. If they hurt, you hurt. If they cry, you cry with them and comfort them. If they need help, you are there to assist. You will do anything for them. You have their best interest at heart. You want to see them grow and mature and fulfill all their hopes and dreams.

Our Messiah feels the same way about us. He wants us to walk in the fullness of His plan for us. At every step, no matter where we are or what we need, He will fill it!

Luke 6:21-23 KJV Blessed [are ye] that hunger now: for ye shall be filled. Blessed [are ye] that weep now: for ye shall laugh. (22) Blessed are ye, when men shall hate you, and when they shall separate you [from their company], and shall reproach [you], and cast out your name as evil, for the Son of man's sake. (23) Rejoice ye in that day, and leap for joy: for, behold, your reward [is] great in heaven: for in the like manner did their fathers unto the prophets.

Exodus 6:6-7 KJV Wherefore say unto the children of Israel, I [am] the LORD, and I will bring you out from under the burdens of the Egyptians, and I will rid you out of their bondage, and I will redeem you with a stretched out arm, and with great judgments: (7) And I will take you to me for a people, and I will be to you a God: and ye shall know that I [am] the LORD your God, which bringeth you out from under the burdens of the Egyptians.

Psalms 55:22 HNV Cast your burden on the LORD, and he will sustain you. He will never allow the righteous to be moved.

Isaiah 58:6 KJV [Is] not this the fast that I have chosen? to loose the bands of wickedness, to undo the heavy burdens, and to let the oppressed go free, and that ye break every yoke?

Galatians 6:1-2 HNV Brothers, even if a man is caught in some fault, you who are spiritual must restore such a one in a spirit of gentleness; looking to yourself so that you also aren't tempted. (2) Bear one another's burdens, and so fulfill the Torah of Messiah.

    The Father does not want us to be bogged down and burdened. He wants to help us bear the burdens we face. Throughout the word we can find an emphasis on meeting with the Father and resting in Him. He is not burdensome, He wants us to come to the realization that He will come to those who call upon Him for help.

Jeremiah 17:21 KJV Thus saith the LORD; Take heed to yourselves, and bear no burden on the sabbath day, nor bring [it] in by the gates of Jerusalem;

But, what about those who continue to say that He is a burden, or that following Him is a burden?

Jeremiah 23:33-40 HNV When this people, or the prophet, or a Kohen, shall ask you, saying, What is the burden of the LORD? then shall you tell them, What burden! I will cast you off, says the LORD. (34) As for the prophet, and the Kohen, and the people, who shall say, The burden of the LORD, I will even punish that man and his house. (35) Thus shall you say everyone to his neighbor, and everyone to his brother, What has the LORD answered? and, What has the LORD spoken? (36) The burden of the LORD shall you mention no more: for every man's own word shall be his burden; for you have perverted the words of the living God, of the LORD of Armies our God. (37) Thus shall you say to the prophet, What has the LORD answered you? and, What has the LORD spoken? (38) But if you say, The burden of the LORD; therefore thus says the LORD: Because you say this word, The burden of the LORD, and I have sent to you, saying, You shall not say, The burden of the LORD; (39) therefore, behold, I will utterly forget you, and I will cast you off, and the city that I gave to you and to your fathers, away from my presence: (40) and I will bring an everlasting reproach on you, and a perpetual shame, which shall not be forgotten.

The Father takes His word seriously. He wants to give us life, His life. We say that we want the life that He gives and then we try to work ourselves out of it. The Father wants us to rest in Him! Come to the Father and He will reveal His rest to you and bring you to rest in it.

Exodus 23:9-12 HNV "You shall not oppress an alien, for you know the heart of an alien, seeing you were aliens in the land of Egypt. (10) "For six years you shall sow your land, and shall gather in its increase, (11) but the seventh year you shall let it rest and lie fallow, that the poor of your people may eat; and what they leave the animal of the field shall eat. In like manner you shall deal with your vineyard and with your olive grove. (12) "Six days you shall do your work, and on the seventh day you shall rest, that your ox and your donkey may have rest, and the son of your handmaid, and the alien may be refreshed.

Exodus 33:13-14 KJV Now therefore, I pray thee, if I have found grace in thy sight, shew me now thy way, that I may know thee, that I may find grace in thy sight: and consider that this nation [is] thy people. (14) And he said, My presence shall go [with thee], and I will give thee rest.

Exodus 35:2 HNV 'Six days shall work be done, but on the seventh day there shall be a holy day for you, a Shabbat of solemn rest to the LORD: whoever does any work in it shall be put to death.

The Shabbat (Sabbath), is the seventh day of the week, the day of rest. We were designed and fashioned to take a break at the appropriate time. This is a time to consecrate as Holy and rest in the word. It is a time given for us to meet with the Father, an appointment with Him. The Creator of Heaven and Earth wants to set up an ongoing weekly appointment with you. At this time spent with Him you will cultivate your relationship and deepen in your love. This is a time to put all other pursuits aside and come to the table to sit down and spend an undistracted, focused time with the one you love.

In this day and age we are in, how often do we put everything else down and just be still and know that He is God? Not worrying about the bills, the kids, the job, the house, the commitments and the list can go on and on. This is a time to cast off the things of the world that can distract us and focus on what really matters. Understand that when I say the world, I am not speaking about sin here. I mean the day to day life that you have to live in this world. We do have to live a life in this world, and because of that, there are necessary things that we need to do in order to make that happen. We need a job, a place to have a roof over our heads, food, etc. To work a job is not a sin. We may not like it, but it is not sin.

When we come to the Shabbat, it is time to put the work down. The work will be there when this time is over. That's part of consecrating something, it has a specific set apart purpose and will not be used for anything but that purpose. Just as you were consecrated to YHWH, He has things consecrated for you and Him. One of those things is Shabbat. This is not a time for us to go out and do what we want and tell the Father "well, you can come if you want." We can't go to the monster truck rally and tell Him He is welcome to come if He wishes and if not, "we will see you when we get back." This is a time that is set apart for you to come in to what the Father wants, to follow His desires and not our own.

He knows what we need and what is best for us. As we seek after Him with all our heart, soul and spirit, we will be refreshed and revived. Isaiah fifty eight addresses what is to be done on the Shabbat.

Isaiah 58:13-14 CJB
- "If you hold back your foot on Shabbat from pursuing *your own interests*
- on *my* holy day;
- if you call Shabbat a delight,
- Adonai's holy day,
- worth honoring;
- then honor it
- by *not doing your* usual things
- or *pursuing your* interests
- or *speaking about them*.
- (14) **If** you do, *you will find delight* in Adonai –
- I will make you ride on the heights of the land
- *and feed you* with the heritage of your ancestor Ya`akov,
- for the *mouth of Adonai* has spoken."

This is a time to pursue the Father, not a time to just relax from the week. This is a time to rest in Him. Think about the above passage. It tells us that we should pursue the Fathers interests, and call them a delight. He also says that *we will be fed* with the heritage of Jacob (Israel)! This is emphasized by the statement that the mouth of the LORD spoke it!

This is the theme for this book. What is the heritage of Israel? The heritage of Israel is the word of YHWH! That is reiterated by saying the "mouth of Adonai". What came from the mouth of Adonai? The word of Adonai! We should receive the heritage that we were given by the Father. As believers in Yeshua HaMoshiach, we are grafted in to Israel and to the promises thereof. I will stress this point, ***we did not replace Israel*!** **We are a *part of* Israel!**

Romans 11:16-27 HNV If the first fruit is holy, so is the lump. If the root is holy, so are the branches. (17) But if

some of the branches were broken off, and you, being a wild olive,
- were grafted in **_among_** them,
- and became partaker **_with them_** of the root and of the richness of the olive tree;
- (18) don't boast over the branches. But if you boast,
- it is not you who support the root,
- but the root supports you.

(19) You will say then, "Branches were broken off, that I might be grafted in." (20) True; by their unbelief they were broken off, and you stand by your faith. Don't be conceited, but fear; (21) for if God didn't spare the natural branches, neither will he spare you. (22) See then the goodness and severity of God. _Toward those who fell,_ severity; but toward you, goodness, if you continue in his goodness; _otherwise you also will be cut off_. (23) They also, if they don't continue in their unbelief, **_will be grafted in_**, for God is able to graft them in again. (24) For _if you were cut out_ of that which is by nature a wild olive tree, _and were grafted_ contrary to nature into a good olive tree, how much more will these, which are the natural branches, be grafted into their own olive tree? (25) For I don't desire, brothers, to have you ignorant of this mystery, so that you won't be wise in your own conceits, that a partial hardening has happened to Yisra'el, until the fullness of the Gentiles has come in, (26) and so **all Yisra'el will be saved.** Even as it is written, "There will come out of Tziyon the Deliverer, and he will turn away ungodliness from Ya`akov. (27) _This is my covenant to them_, when I will take away their sins."

You cannot change your heritage. You will pass along your heritage to your children. You can add to the legacy of your heritage. But you cannot change what has already happened. The Father wants to pass along His heritage to His children. Are we willing to receive it wholeheartedly? We come to Him and accept and receive the heritage of our heavenly Father. The heritage we have received will be from our earthly forefathers, or our heavenly Father. We have received our heritage from our fathers all the way back to Adam.

Adam, the first man, caused sin to enter into the world and passed it down through the bloodline. We have been given an opportunity to come and be adopted by our heavenly Father thereby gaining a new heritage!

Jeremiah 16:19 HNV   LORD, my strength, and my stronghold, and my refuge in the day of affliction, to you shall the nations come from the ends of the earth, and shall say, Our fathers have inherited nothing but lies, [even] vanity and things in which there is no profit.

When we come to the Father, we must trade in our worldly inheritance for the Heavenly inheritance. In other words, we trade in our idolatry, our concepts and ideas of who we think God is, for who He reveals himself to be. One of the ways He revealed Himself was by His word. His word reveals His character and the inheritance He is passing on to His children. One part of the inheritance is the Shabbat. Why do we fight so hard against being told to stop running around all over the place and rest?

Is it burdensome to not work? Is it burdensome to read the Scripture? Is it a burden to have a conversation with the One that you love? Is it a burden to walk along a path with the One you love, holding hands along the way? We don't like being told what to do, even if it is for our benefit. We are like children who are tired and cranky, unwilling to listen to what is best for us and rest.

Do we come to the Father, or serve Him, grudgingly? Think back to the verse we just read in Isaiah fifty eight. How often do we do something not because our heart is in it, but because we know it's what the Father would want? Do we give in because we know that it would be best? Is our heart really in it?

Deuteronomy 28:47-48 HNV Because you didn't serve the LORD your God *with joyfulness, and with gladness of heart,* by reason of the abundance of all things; (48) therefore shall you serve your enemies whom the LORD shall send against you, in hunger, and in thirst, and in nakedness, and in want of all things: and he shall put a yoke of iron on your neck, until he have destroyed you.

We need to have it in our hearts to serve the Father. I am not saying that in order to be redeemed or born again you must gain it by your service. What I _am_ saying is; _because you are redeemed_, you will serve Him. Part of serving Him means we do what He says, when He says it. The Father is telling us he wants to meet with us and we are responding " Alright, I will get around to meeting with you at my convenience."

I have never seen or heard so much opposition in the body of Messiah as when you mention Shabbat or food. Why do we fight so hard to _not_ rest? The fact is, we all need refreshing and rest. So, if we are supposed to rest, when do we rest?

Exodus 16:23-30 HNV He said to them, "This is that which the LORD has spoken, 'Tomorrow is a solemn rest, a holy Shabbat to the LORD. Bake that which you want to bake, and boil that which you want to boil; and all that remains over lay up for yourselves to be kept until the morning.'" (24) They laid it up until the morning, as Moshe asked, and it didn't become foul, neither was there any worm in it. (25) Moshe said, "Eat that today, for today is a Shabbat to the LORD. Today you shall not find it in the field. (26) Six days you shall gather it, but _on the seventh day is the Shabbat_. In it there shall be none." (27) It happened on the seventh day, that some of the people went out to gather, and they found none. (28) The LORD said to Moshe, "How long do you refuse to keep my mitzvot and my laws? (29) Behold, because _the LORD has given you the Shabbat_, therefore he gives you on the sixth day the bread of two days. Everyone stay in his place. Let no one go out of his place _on the seventh day_." (30) So the people _rested on the seventh day_.

The most common argument for the above reference is; which day is the seventh day? This is another area where the richness of Hebrew comes in to the picture. There are some things that don't translate well into English. An example of what is lost in translation is the days of the week. In Hebrew what we would call "Sunday" is called literally the "first day". This needs to be understood in order to comprehend why the seventh day is Shabbat.

The days of the week in Hebrew in comparison to the English/ Gregorian /Julian Calendar are listed in the chart below.

Hebrew	Transliteration	Meaning	Gregorian equivalent
יום ראשון	Yom Reshown	First Day	Sunday
יום שני	Yom Shenee	Second Day	Monday
יום שלישי	Yom Shleeshee	Third Day	Tuesday
יום רביעי	Yom Reve'ee	Fourth Day	Wednesday
יום חמישי	Yom Chameshee	Fifth Day	Thursday
יום ששי	Yom Sheshe	Sixth Day	Friday
שבת	**Shabbat**	**Rest**	Saturday

Each day of the week is named by its' number. The Sabbath is named and called Shabbat! There is no way it can be another day because if we were to call it another day, we would be changing its' name, thereby changing the calendar that was put in place by YHWH!

Daniel 7:25 KJV And he (the anti-Christ /anti-Messiah) shall speak [great] words against the most High, and shall wear out the saints of the most High, <u>and think to change times and laws</u>: and they shall be given into his hand until a time and times and the dividing of time.

The next question would be, "If Shabbat is the seventh day, why does it start on Friday night?" The answer is found in the first chapter of Genesis (B'resheit in Hebrew). The Biblical reckoning of time lists the evening first. This sound confusing to most but that is the way it was laid out in scripture. In order to understand what constitutes "one day", we need to define the parameters of what "one day" is.

Genesis 1:5 KJV And God called the light Day, and the darkness he called Night. And the evening and the morning were the first day.

What is interesting to note here is; in the original Hebrew, which is what Torah was written in, does not say **_first_** day! If it said first day it would say Yom Reshown. It does not, it says literally "**_one_** day" which would be, Yom Echad! Alright you may be saying to yourself, "So, what's the difference?" The difference is that saying first day would make sense to us, seeing that it literally was the first day, but something had to happen here. We need to let Scripture be used to define Scripture. There had to be something established here. Before the Father could tell you anything about days of the week, you first have to know what a day is! The passage is giving us the definition and parameters of what is one day.

Remember, in our earlier example of Manna, Israel was told that they would receive food from Heaven but when they saw it they said "What is it?". In order to understand the reckoning of time, we need the Father, the One who created time, to define it for us. He did so in the first chapter of Genesis.

Once we have the definition of when, we could address the why. We could easily say because the Father said so and leave it at that. The Father, however, does give Shabbat a purpose. Not only was it given for us to rest, it was given as a sign. It's ironic if you think about it. We hear people cry out for the Father to give them a sign. He said He already gave us a sign. It is a sign that still exists today!

Exodus 31:12-17 HNV The LORD spoke to Moshe, saying, (13) "Speak also to the children of Yisra'el, saying, 'Most certainly you shall _keep my Shabbatot_: for _it is a sign between me and you_ throughout your generations; that you may know that I am the LORD who sanctifies you. (14) You shall keep the Shabbat therefore; for it is holy to you. Everyone who profanes it shall surely be put to death; for whoever does any work therein, that soul shall be cut off from among his people.

- (15) Six days shall work be done, but on the seventh day is a Shabbat
- of solemn rest,
- holy to the LORD.
- Whoever does any work on the day of Shabbat shall surely be put to death.
- (16) Therefore the children of Yisra'el shall keep the Shabbat,
- to observe the Shabbat
- throughout their generations,
- for a ***perpetual covenant***.
- (17) ***It is a sign***
- between me and the children of Yisra'el
- ***forever***;
- for in six days the LORD made heaven and earth, and on the seventh day he rested, and was refreshed.'"

Shabbat was given to us to observe and keep. It would stand as a sign of covenant and it is stated that it was a sign forever. The Hebrew for sign would be the word:

H226

אוֹת

'ôth

oth

Probably from H225 (in the sense of *appearing*); a *signal* (literally or figuratively), as a *flag, beacon, monument, omen, prodigy, evidence*, etc.: - mark, miracle, (en-) sign, token.

The Shabbat was given to us as evidence or a mark or an ensign. I find ensign to be a curious definition. Websters defines ensign as:

Ensign
EN'SIGN, n. en'sine. [L. insigne, insignia, from signum, a mark impressed, a sign.]

1. The flag or banner of a military band; a banner of colors; a standard; a figured cloth or piece of silk, attached to a staff, and usually with figures, colors or arms thereon, borne by an officer at the head of a company, troop or other band.
2. Any signal to assemble or to give notice.
He will lift up an ensign to the nations. Isa 5.
Ye shall be left as an ensign on a hill. Isa 30.
3. A badge; a mark of distinction, rank or office; as ensigns of power or virtue.
4. The officer who carries the flag or colors, being the lowest commissioned officer in a company of infantry.
5. Naval ensign, is a large banner hoisted on a staff and carried over the poop or stern of a ship; used to distinguish ships of different nations, or to characterize different equadrons of the same navy.

Do you see what sign the Father is giving you? You will keep the Shabbat as a rallying point or banner in order to distinguish you and set you apart from different nations. Which kingdom banner are you rallying under?

Ezekiel 20:10-13 HNV So I caused them to go forth out of the land of Egypt, and brought them into the wilderness. (11) I gave them my statutes, and shown them my ordinances, which if a man do, he shall live in them. (12) Moreover also I gave them my Shabbatot, to be a sign between me and them, that they might know that I am the LORD who sanctifies them. (13) But the house of Yisra'el rebelled against me in the wilderness: they didn't walk in my statutes, and they rejected my ordinances, which if a man keep, he shall live in them; and my Shabbatot they greatly profaned. Then I said I would pour out my wrath on them in the wilderness, to consume them.

In Scripture, we see Yeshua and the Apostles going to the synagogues on Shabbat. This is not against the command to rest. Remember we are to rest in Him. That means that we get into the word and the community of the Messiah. Leviticus 23:1-4 tells us that Shabbat is a Holy Convocation. That means it is a Holy Gathering! <u>GO</u> to the synagogues on Shabbat and read the word, study it, and worship with your brothers and sisters.

Leviticus 23:1-4 HNV The LORD spoke to Moshe, saying, (2) "Speak to the children of Yisra'el, and tell them, 'The set feasts of the LORD, which you shall proclaim to be holy convocations, even these are **my** set feasts. (3) "'Six days shall work be done: but on the seventh day is a Shabbat of solemn rest, a holy convocation; you shall do no manner of work. It is a **Shabbat to the LORD** in all your dwellings. (4) "'**These are the set feasts of the LORD**, even holy convocations, which *you shall proclaim* **in their appointed** season.

We cannot proclaim any of these times other than when the Father designated them. Since He is the same today, yesterday and forever, and He doesn't change, He did not change any of them! So, we see that Yeshua and others were found in the synagogues on Shabbat.

Mark 6:2 KJV And when the sabbath day was come, he began to teach in the synagogue: and many hearing *him were astonished, saying, From whence hath this man these things? and what wisdom is this which is given unto him, that even such mighty works are wrought by his hands?*

Luke 4:16 KJV And he came to Nazareth, where he had been brought up: and, as his custom was, he went into the synagogue on the sabbath day, and stood up for to read.

Luke 4:31 KJV And came down to Capernaum, a city of Galilee, and taught them on the sabbath days.

Luke 6:6 KJV And it came to pass also on another sabbath, that he entered into the synagogue and taught: and there was a man whose right hand was withered.

Luke 13:10 KJV And he was teaching in one of the synagogues on the sabbath.

Acts 13:14 KJV But when they departed from Perga, they came to Antioch in Pisidia, and went into the synagogue on the sabbath day, and sat down.

Acts 13:44 KJV And the next sabbath day came almost the whole city together to hear the word of God.

Acts 15:21 KJV For Moses of old time hath in every city them that preach him, being read in the synagogues every sabbath day.

Acts 18:4 KJV And he reasoned in the synagogue every sabbath, and persuaded the Jews and the Greeks.

So, we see that there remains a Shabbat for the children of YHWH! He did not take it away from us! We just haven't seen it revealed so that we could walk in it.

Hebrews 4:1-12 HNV Let us fear therefore, lest perhaps anyone of you should seem to have come short of a promise of entering into his rest. (2) For indeed we have had good news preached to us, even as they also did, but the word they heard didn't profit them, because it wasn't mixed with faith by those who heard. (3) For we who have believed do enter into that rest, even as he has said, "As I swore in my wrath, they will not enter into my rest;" although the works were finished from the foundation of the world. (4) For he has said this somewhere about the seventh day, "God rested on the seventh day from all his works;" (5) and in this place again, "They will not enter into my rest." (6) Seeing therefore it remains that some should enter therein, and they to whom the good news was before preached failed to enter in because of disobedience, (7) he again defines a certain day, today, saying through David so long a time afterward (just as has been said), "Today if you will hear his voice, don't harden your hearts." (8) For if Yehoshua had given them rest, he would not have spoken afterward of another day. (9) There remains therefore a Shabbat rest for the people of God. (10) For he who has entered into his rest has himself also rested from his works, as God did from his. (11) Let us therefore give diligence to enter into that rest, lest anyone fall after the same example of disobedience. (12) For the word of God is living, and active, and sharper than any two-edged sword, and piercing even to the dividing of soul and spirit, of both joints and marrow, and is able to discern the thoughts and intentions of the heart.

The Father literally said, that keeping Shabbat is a mark of distinction for you! We see from the passage in Hebrews that it takes trust or faith to receive and keep the Shabbat. Have you received the mark of distinction as a sign? This word for sign would be used in the same way that we see a wedding ring on someone's finger and immediately know that they belong to someone else.

The first time this word for "sign" is used in scripture is in Genesis 1:14.
Genesis 1:14-19 HNV God said, "Let there be lights in the expanse of sky to divide the day from the night; and **_let them be for signs, and for seasons_**, and for days and years; (15) and let them be for lights in the expanse of sky to give light on the earth;" and it was so. (16) God made the two great lights: the greater light to rule the day, and the lesser light to rule the night. He also made the stars. (17) God set them in the expanse of sky to give light to the earth, (18) and to rule over the day and over the night, and to divide the light from the darkness. God saw that it was good. (19) There was evening and there was morning, a fourth day.

The first time this word was used, it was to reckon time and the Biblical calendar. The lights in the sky were to order the days, months and years. It also states seasons. It's worth mentioning here that all the feasts and festivals of Scripture use the same word that is defined here as seasons.
That word is Mo'edim

H4150

מוֹעֵד מֹעֵד מוֹעָדָה

moʻêd moʻêd môʻâdâh

mo-ade', mo-ade', mo-aw-daw'

From H3259; properly an *appointment*, that is, a fixed *time* or season; specifically a *festival*; conventionally a *year*; by implication, an *assembly* (as convened for a definite purpose); technically the *congregation*; by extension, the *place of meeting*; also a *signal* (as appointed beforehand): - appointed (sign, time), (place of, solemn) assembly, congregation, (set, solemn) feast, (appointed, due) season, solemn (-ity), synagogue, (set) time (appointed).

The appointed times of Scripture that the Father set in order to meet with us, are seasons of appointments that He intends to keep, whether we keep them or not. All of the Moedim (appointments) of the LORD are in Leviticus 23, for your further study. We cannot walk outside in the middle of August and declare that we don't like the heat, so we will now change the month of August into winter. Did our declaration make the summer heat cease? We do not have the authority to change what the Father set in place. The only time that we see change as burdensome is when we don't want to change.

We may have many reasons for not changing. In the end, will they stand? Do we belong to us or to the One who redeemed us? Have we received His mark of distinction that sets us apart? I am not speaking of your salvation through the Messiah. I am speaking of you living your life set apart, consecrated to the Father. When you decide to live your life set apart and follow the banner that was raised for you, you will learn how to walk in the Spirit of the LORD!

Chapter Six

THE REFRESHING OF THE SPIRIT

Galatians 5:16 KJV [This] I say then, Walk in the Spirit, and ye shall not fulfil the lust of the flesh.

Acts 3:19-21 HNV "Repent therefore, and turn again, that your sins may be blotted out, so that there may come times of refreshing from the presence of the Lord, (20) and that he may send Messiah Yeshua, who was ordained for you before, (21) whom heaven must receive until the times of restoration of all things, which God spoke long ago by the mouth of his holy prophets.

Refreshing comes from the presence of the Father. Part of that refreshing is restoration. What does it mean to restore something? My Father used to restore old cars. He would look all over for a car that he wanted. After all, if he didn't want it, why restore it? Once he found what he was looking for, he would purchase it from the owner. At the time of purchase, these cars were run down and needed work! They were rusty. They wouldn't run. Some didn't have engines in them. They needed major work.

After the car was purchased, the next task was to get it home. Do you think that in order to get to the destination, he pulled out a bottle of wax and started to polish the car? No, the first step was to see if it would start. Did it have gas in it? Did it have oil in it? Were all the belts and hoses in good order? In some cases, the cars were so bad that they had to be towed home and put in the garage.

Once they were in the garage, all the other internal parts were examined to see if they needed either replaced or repaired. When they were running decently, the tires were replaced in order to get them on the road. They didn't look the best, but they could <u>run</u>! The first car I drove, after getting my license, was a 1957 Ford Fairlane 500. Next came a 1967 Ford Mustang.

These were real cars! They had a lot of "heart" and character. But they needed an awful lot of work. I have come to realize that a lot of the "heart" I felt and saw in these old cars, was the "heart" that my father put into them in order to restore them. One of the ways that my father showed me that he cared for me was the work and preparation he put into the vehicle I would be driving.

The process to get them on the road was a long road in and of itself. My father poured his heart and soul into the restoration of these vehicles that would carry him around wherever he went. Hours led to days, days led to a month and one month led to many months. When the process was finished, they were as beautiful on the outside as they were on the inside. The sense of pride and accomplishment he would feel as he got behind the wheel of one of those vehicles was worth all of the work.

He would put a lot of work into those cars. Especially since He knew they would carry his son. He wanted them to not only carry his son, he wanted them to represent him and the work that he put into them. Do you see the parallels between the restoration of those vehicles and our restoration?

Webster's 1828 dictionary defines restoration as:

Restoration
RESTORA'TION, n. [L. restauro.]

1. The act of replacing in a former state.
Behold the different climes agree, rejoicing in thy restoration.
So we speak of the restoration of a man to his office, or to a good standing in society.

2. Renewal; revival; re-establishment; as the restoration of friendship between enemies; the restoration of peace after war; the restoration of a declining commerce.
3. Recovery; renewal of health and soundness; as restoration from sickness or from insanity.
4. Recovery from a lapse or any bad state; as the restoration of man from apostasy.
5. In theology, universal restoration, the final recovery of all men from sin and alienation from God, to a state of happiness; universal salvation.
6. In England, the return of king Charles II in 1660, and the re-establishment of monarchy.

When the Father speaks of restoration for you, it will be better than when you started. Restoration for you is to be restored to the will of the Father. He will restore you to His plan, His purpose, His word, His kingdom and all of the promises you were intended to walk in from the beginning. We are all familiar with and have heard the story of Job.

Job 42:10 HNV The LORD turned the captivity of Iyov, when he prayed for his friends. The LORD gave Iyov twice as much as he had before.

Job 42:12 HNV So the LORD blessed the latter end of Iyov more than his beginning. He had fourteen thousand sheep, six thousand camels, one thousand yoke of oxen, and a thousand female donkeys.

Job's restoration was doubled and blessed by the Father. The ultimate restoration will be when we see Him face to face!

We do not have to wait until we die to have the restoration of the Father in our lives. He wants us to walk in the Kingdom of Heaven NOW! We often hear people talk of the "by and by". There's nothing wrong with looking forward to the great reward when we will see Him face to face. Just don't live there! A great part of the restoration to us, is learning how to walk in the Spirit of YHWH in our lives now.

Yeshua told Nicodemus that in order to see the Kingdom of God, you must see it by the Spirit.

John 3:1-7 KJV There was a man of the Pharisees, named Nicodemus, a ruler of the Jews: (2) The same came to Jesus by night, and said unto him, Rabbi, we know that thou art a teacher come from God: for no man can do these miracles that thou doest, except God be with him. (3) Jesus answered and said unto him, Verily, verily, I say unto thee, Except a man be born again, he cannot see the kingdom of God. (4) Nicodemus saith unto him, How can a man be born when he is old? can he enter the second time into his mother's womb, and be born? (5) Jesus answered, Verily, verily, I say unto thee, Except a man be born of water and [of] the Spirit, he cannot enter into the kingdom of God. (6) That which is born of the flesh is flesh; and that which is born of the Spirit is spirit. (7) Marvel not that I said unto thee, Ye must be born again.

Look at verse three above. A person must be born again to see the Kingdom. We need to stop trying to see the Kingdom in our own flesh (our old nature – our selfish and worldly desires). If we are to see the Kingdom of Heaven, we need to learn how to walk in the Spirit of YHWH.

Luke 17:20-21 HNV Being asked by the Perushim when the Kingdom of God would come, he answered them, "The Kingdom of God doesn't come with observation; (21) neither will they say, 'Look, here!' or, 'Look, there!' for behold, the Kingdom of God is within you."

The word in verse twenty one for among is actually the Greek word for Within!

G1787 - ἐ ντός– entos -*en-tos'*

From G1722; *inside* (adverb or noun): - within.

These Scriptures say that we will not see the Kingdom because we are looking in this world, and to the world's values and ways, for the Kingdom.

We cannot approach the Father by the world's standards. We must come to Him and His Kingdom, His way. If we are to walk in, or even see, the Kingdom of Heaven we will need to see it through His eyes!

Matthew 3:1-3 KJV In those days came John the Baptist, preaching in the wilderness of Judaea, (2) And saying, Repent ye: for the kingdom of heaven is at hand. (3) For this is he that was spoken of by the prophet Esaias, saying, The voice of one crying in the wilderness, Prepare ye the way of the Lord, make his paths straight.

Drawing into the Kingdom requires repentance. Repentance is turning from the old nature and the desires of those things that work against the Kingdom, and turning to the Father and His Spirit. You may not be able to see the Spirit or the Kingdom with your natural eyes but you can see the fruit, or product, of it.

Galatians 5:16-25 HNV But I say, walk by the Spirit, and you won't fulfill the lust of the flesh. (17) For the flesh lusts against the Spirit, and the Spirit against the flesh; and these are contrary to one another, that you may not do the things that you desire. (18) But if you are led by the Spirit, you are not under the law. (19) Now the works of the flesh are obvious, which are: adultery, sexual immorality, uncleanness, lustfulness, (20) idolatry, sorcery, hatred, strife, jealousies, outbursts of anger, rivalries, divisions, heresies, (21) envyings, murders, drunkenness, orgies, and things like these; of which I forewarn you, even as I also forewarned you, that those who practice such things will not inherit the Kingdom of God. (22) But the fruit of the Spirit is love, joy, shalom, patience, kindness, goodness, faith, (23) gentleness, and self-control. Against such things there is no law. (24) Those who belong to Messiah have crucified the flesh with its passions and lusts. (25) If we live by the Spirit, let's also walk by the Spirit.

When we turn to the Father and walk in His word, we will be walking in the kingdom of Heaven. We will have dual citizenship, if you will. This is when you live in one country, or kingdom, and at the same time you belong to another. In one manner of speaking it is similar to that. We may live in this world but we belong to another. In our case, one kingdom actually takes precedence over another.

We are ambassadors, so to speak. No matter where we are in this world, we represent the Kingdom of Heaven. We are subject to, and operate by, the rules of our Kingdom. The soil we walk on, no matter where it may be, is declared to be the ground of the Kingdom. This concept has been mentioned in scripture more than once.

Genesis 13:14-17 HNV The LORD said to Avram, after Lot was separated from him, "Now, lift up your eyes, and look from the place where you are, northward and southward and eastward and westward, (15) for all the land which you see, I will give to you, and to your offspring forever. (16) I will make your offspring as the dust of the earth, so that if a man can number the dust of the earth, then your seed may also be numbered. (17) Arise, walk through the land in the length of it and in the breadth of it; for I will give it to you."

Deuteronomy 11:22-28 HNV For if you shall diligently keep all this mitzvah which I command you, to do it, to love the LORD your God, to walk in all his ways, and to cleave to him; (23) then will the LORD drive out all these nations from before you, and you shall dispossess nations greater and mightier than yourselves. (24) Every place whereon the sole of your foot shall tread shall be yours: from the wilderness, and Levanon, from the river, the river Perat, even to the hinder sea shall be your border. (25) There shall no man be able to stand before you: the LORD your God shall lay the fear of you and the dread of you on all the land that you shall tread on, as he has spoken to you. (26) Behold, I set before you this day a blessing and a curse: (27) the blessing, if you shall listen to the mitzvot of the LORD your God, which I command you this day; (28) and the curse, if you shall not listen to the mitzvot of the LORD your God, but turn aside out of the way which I command you this day, to go after other gods, which you have not known.

Joshua 1:3-9 HNV I have given you every place that the sole of your foot will tread on, as I told Moshe. (4) From the wilderness, and this Levanon, even to the great river, the river Perat, all the land of the Chitti, and to the great sea toward the going down of the sun, shall be your border. (5) No man will be able to stand before you all the days of your life. As I was with Moshe, so I will be with you. I will not fail you nor forsake you. (6) Be strong and of good courage; for you shall cause this people to inherit the land which I swore to their fathers to give them. (7) Only be strong and very courageous, to observe to do according to all the law, which Moshe my servant commanded you. Don't turn from it to the right hand or to the left, that you may have good success wherever you go. (8) This scroll of the Torah shall not depart out of your mouth, but you shall meditate on it day and night, that you may observe to do according to all that is written therein: for then you shall make your way prosperous, and then you shall have good success. (9) Haven't I commanded you? Be strong and of good courage. Don't be afraid, neither be dismayed: for the LORD your God is with you wherever you go.

We see from these passages that walking in the Kingdom of Heaven and receiving the benefits of it, go hand in hand with abiding by the rules of that Kingdom.

Walking in the Kingdom requires us to walk in the Spirit of YHWH. We walk in the Spirit of YHWH when we walk in His word. The Father tells us that He gives us His spirit to equip us and enable us to walk in His word! The Hebrew word for spirit is Ruach.

H7307 --רוּחַ -rûach- *roo'-akh*

From H7306; *wind*; by resemblance *breath*, that is, a sensible (or even violent) exhalation; figuratively *life, anger, unsubstantiality*; by extension a *region* of the sky; by resemblance *spirit*, but only of a rational being (including its expression and functions): - air, anger, blast, breath, X cool, courage, mind, X quarter, X side, spirit ([-ual]), tempest, X vain, ([whirl-]) wind (-y).

H7306- רוּחַ -rûach -*roo'-akh*

A primitive root; properly to *blow*, that is, *breathe*; only (literally) to *smell* or (by implication *perceive* (figuratively to *anticipate, enjoy*): - accept, smell, X touch, make of quick understanding.

    The prophet Ezekiel confirms that the Spirit of YHWH is given to us, so that we will be equipped to walk in the ways, word and commandments of YHWH. Look at and examine all the promises and declarations in the following passage from Ezekiel chapter thirty six.

Ezekiel 36:22-30 HNV Therefore tell the house of Yisra'el, Thus says the Lord GOD: I don't do [this] for your sake, house of Yisra'el, but for my holy name, which you have profaned among the nations, where you went. (23) I will sanctify my great name, which has been profaned among the nations, which you have profaned in the midst of them; and the nations shall know that I am the LORD, says the Lord GOD, when
- I shall be sanctified
- in you before their eyes.
- (24) For I will take you from among the nations,
- and gather you out of all the countries,
- and will bring you into your own land.
- (25) I will sprinkle clean water on you,
- and you shall be clean:
- from all your filthiness,
- and from all your idols,
- will I cleanse you.
- (26) A new heart also will I give you,
- and a new spirit will I put within you;
- and I will take away the stony heart out of your flesh,
- and I will give you a heart of flesh.
- (27) I will put my Spirit within you,
- and cause you to walk in my statutes,
- and you shall keep my ordinances,
- and do them.

- (28) You shall dwell in the land that I gave to your fathers; and you shall be my people, and I will be your God.
- (29) I will save you from all your uncleanness:
- and I will call for the grain, and will multiply it,
- and lay no famine on you.
- (30) I will multiply the fruit of the tree, and the increase of the field, that you may receive no more the reproach of famine among the nations.

To fully understand what this passage of Scripture is saying to us, we will need to break it down into sections.

In the first section the Father says that what He is about to do is for the sake of His Holy Name. A person's name is an important thing in the ancient Hebrew mindset. When you called someone by their name you were saying more than a word to get someone's attention, you were speaking of their character or the character of the person they were named after. The Hebrew word for name is "Shem":

H8034- שׁם -shêm -*shame*

A primitive word (perhaps rather from H7760 through the idea of definite and conspicuous *position*; compare H8064); an *appellation*, as a mark or memorial of individuality; by implication *honor, authority, character:* - + base, [in-] fame [-ous], name (-d), renown, report.

When you spoke to (or of) a person, you were identifying something about that person. You were revealing something about them. One good example of this would be the prophet Zechariah. His name was actually a compound word from two other words: Zachar and Yah.

H2142- זָכַר -zâkar -*zaw-kar'*

A primitive root; properly to *mark* (so as to be recognized), that is, to *remember*; by implication to *mention*; also (as denominative from H2145) to *be male:* - X burn [incense], X earnestly, be male, (make) mention (of), be mindful, recount, record (-er), remember, make to be remembered, bring (call, come, keep, put) to (in) remembrance, X still, think on, X well.

H3050 –יָהּ -yâhh -*yaw*

Contracted for H3068, and meaning the same; *Jah*, the sacred name: - Jah, the Lord, most vehement. Cp. names in "-iah," "-jah."

So, the prophet Zechariah's name means God remembers or God marks! In the passage before from Isaiah, it is declared that the name or Character of the Father has been profaned among the nations and we did it!

What does it mean to say that we have profaned the name of YHWH? There are many scriptures to define this. I will list only a few of them.

Leviticus 18:21 KJV And thou shalt not let any of thy seed pass through [the fire] to Molech, neither shalt thou profane the name of thy God: I [am] the LORD.

One way that we profane the Name is if we give up our children to idolatry. We also would profane the name if we swear falsely by His name. Have you ever heard the expression "I swear to God" when you knew someone was not telling the whole truth?

Leviticus 19:12 HNV "'You shall not swear by my name falsely, and profane the name of your God. I am the LORD.

Leviticus 22:31-33 HNV "Therefore you shall keep my mitzvot, and do them. I am the LORD. (32) You shall not profane my holy name, but I will be made holy among the children of Yisra'el. I am the LORD who makes you holy, (33) who brought you out of the land of Egypt, to be your God. I am the LORD."

When we live our life in such a way that people treat each other and the Father as Holy, it is pleasant to the Father. When we live our life in such a way that people will look at us and say "and they say they're a believer" we have potentially profaned the name of our God. When we keep the word of the LORD, it will be wisdom for us, and a testimony to others.

Deuteronomy 4:5-9 HNV Behold, I have taught you statutes and ordinances, even as the LORD my God commanded me, that you should do so in the midst of the land where you go in to possess it. (6) Keep therefore and do them; for this is your wisdom and your understanding in the sight of the peoples, who shall hear all these statutes, and say, Surely this great nation is a wise and understanding people. (7) For what great nation is there, that has a god so near to them, as the LORD our God is whenever we call on him? (8) What great nation is there, that has statutes and ordinances so righteous as all this law, which I set before you this day? (9) Only take heed to yourself, and keep your soul diligently, lest you forget the things which your eyes saw, and lest they depart from your heart all the days of your life; but make them known to your children and your children's children;

Ezekiel 39:7 HNV My holy name will I make known in the midst of my people Yisra'el; neither will I allow my holy name to be profaned any more: and the nations shall know that I am the LORD, the Holy One in Yisra'el.

The next part of Ezekiel 36 is in verse 24:
- I will take you from among the nations,
- and gather you out of all the countries,
- and will bring you into your own land.

We have all come from many nations. We all are in need of being gathered into the Kingdom of Heaven and into the eternal promises given by covenant. We, who would come from all nations (goyim in Hebrew), would come and be grafted into the eternal covenant provisions that the Father made with His children.

Ephesians 2:8-22 HNV for by grace you have been saved through faith, and that not of yourselves; it is the gift of God, (9) not of works, that no one would boast. (10) For we are his workmanship, created in Messiah Yeshua for good works, which God prepared before that we would walk in them. (11) Therefore remember that once you, the Gentiles in the flesh, who are called "uncircumcision" by that which is called "circumcision," (in the flesh, made by hands); (12) that *you were at that time separate from Messiah, alienated from the commonwealth of Yisra'el*, and *strangers from the covenants of the promise*, having no hope and without God in the world. (13) But now in Messiah Yeshua *you who once were far off are made near* in the blood of Messiah. (14) For he is our shalom, who made both one, and broke down the middle wall of partition, (15) having abolished in the flesh the hostility, the Torah of commandments contained in ordinances, *that he might create in himself one new man of the two, making shalom*; (16) and might reconcile them both in one body to God through the cross, having killed the hostility thereby. (17) He came and preached shalom to you who were far off and to those who were near. (18) For through him we both have our access in one Spirit to the Father. (19) So then *you are no longer strangers and foreigners, but*

- ***you are fellow citizens***
- *with the holy ones,*
- *and of the household of God*,

(20) being built on the foundation of the emissaries and prophets, Messiah Yeshua himself being the chief cornerstone; (21) in whom the whole building, fitted together, grows into a holy temple in the Lord; (22) in whom ***you also are built together*** for a habitation of God in the Spirit.

Jeremiah 50:4-6 HNV In those days, and in that time, says the LORD, the children of Yisra'el shall come, they and the children of Yehudah together; they shall go on their way weeping, and shall seek the LORD their God. (5) They shall inquire concerning Tziyon with their faces turned toward it, [saying], Come, and join yourselves to the LORD in an everlasting covenant that shall not be forgotten. (6) My people have been lost sheep: their shepherds have caused them to go astray; they have turned them away on the mountains; they have gone from mountain to hill; they have forgotten their resting place.

Matthew 10:5-7 HNV Yeshua sent these twelve out, and charged them, saying, "Don't go among the Gentiles, and don't enter into any city of the Shomroni. (6) Rather, go to the lost sheep of the house of Yisra'el. (7) As you go, preach, saying, 'The Kingdom of Heaven is at hand!'

Matthew 15:22-28 HNV Behold, a Kena`ani woman came out from those borders, and cried, saying, "Have mercy on me, Lord, you son of David! My daughter is severely demonized!" (23) But he answered her not a word. His talmidim came and begged him, saying, "Send her away; for she cries after us." (24) But he answered, "I wasn't sent to anyone but the lost sheep of the house of Yisra'el." (25) But she came and worshiped him, saying, "Lord, help me." (26) But he answered, "It is not appropriate to take the children's bread and throw it to the dogs." (27) But she said, "Yes, Lord, but even the dogs eat the crumbs which fall from their masters' table." (28) Then Yeshua answered her, "Woman, great is your faith! Be it done to you even as you desire." And her daughter was healed from that hour.

Luke 15:4-7 CJB "If one of you has a hundred sheep and loses one of them, doesn't he leave the other ninety-nine in the desert and go after the lost one until he finds it? (5) When he does find it, he joyfully hoists it onto his shoulders; (6) and when he gets home, he calls his friends and neighbors together and says, 'Come, celebrate with me, because I have found my lost sheep!' (7) I tell you that in the same way, there will be more joy in heaven over one sinner who turns to God from his sins than over ninety-nine righteous people who have no need to repent.

These are promises of re-gathering all of the children who were wayward. All of those who are willing to lay down the idolatry and to come and know Him. If we will turn to the Father and seek after Him, we will soon see that He has sent out search parties to go and minister to all who will seek Him.

Jeremiah 16:12-21 HNV and you have done evil more than your fathers; for, behold, you walk every one after the stubbornness of his evil heart, so that you don't listen to me: (13) therefore will I cast you forth out of this land into the land that you have not known, neither you nor your fathers; and there shall you serve other gods day and night; for I will show you no favor. (14) Therefore, behold, the days come, says the LORD, that it shall no more be said, As the LORD lives, who brought up the children of Yisra'el out of the land of Egypt; (15) but, As the LORD lives, who brought up the children of Yisra'el from the land of the north, and from all the countries where he had driven them. I will bring them again into their land that I gave to their fathers. (16) Behold, I will send for many fishermen, says the LORD, and they shall fish them up; and afterward I will send for many hunters, and they shall hunt them from every mountain, and from every hill, and out of the clefts of the rocks. (17) For my eyes are on all their ways; they are not hidden from my face, neither is their iniquity concealed from my eyes. (18) First I will recompense their iniquity and their sin double, because they have polluted my land with the carcasses of their detestable things, and have filled my inheritance with their abominations. (19) LORD, my strength, and my stronghold, and my refuge in the day of affliction, to you shall the nations come from the ends of the earth, and shall say, Our fathers have inherited nothing but lies, [even] vanity and things in which there is no profit. (20) Shall a man make to himself gods, which yet are no gods? (21) Therefore, behold, I will cause them to know, this once will I cause them to know my hand and my might; and they shall know that my name is the LORD.

Jeremiah 23:1-6 HNV Woe to the shepherds who destroy and scatter the sheep of my pasture! says the LORD. (2) Therefore thus says the LORD, the God of Yisra'el, against the shepherds who feed my people: You have scattered my

(35) and I will bring you into the wilderness of the peoples, and there will I enter into judgment with you face to face. (36) Like as I entered into judgment with your fathers in the wilderness of the land of Egypt, so will I enter into judgment with you, says the Lord GOD. (37) **_I will cause you to pass under the rod, and I will bring you into the bond of the covenant;_** (38) and I will purge out from among you the rebels, and those who disobey against me; I will bring them forth out of the land where they sojourn, but they shall not enter into Eretz-Yisra'el: and you shall know that I am the LORD. (39) As for you, house of Yisra'el, thus says the Lord GOD: Go you, serve everyone his idols, and hereafter also, if you will not listen to me; but my holy name shall you no more profane with your gifts, and with your idols. (40) For in my holy mountain, in the mountain of the height of Yisra'el, says the Lord GOD, there shall all the house of Yisra'el, all of them, serve me in the land: there will I accept them, and there will I require your offerings, and the first fruits of your offerings, with all your holy things.

Ezekiel 28:25-26 HNV Thus says the Lord GOD: When I shall have gathered the house of Yisra'el from the peoples among whom they are scattered, and shall be sanctified in them in the sight of the nations, then shall they dwell in their own land which I gave to my servant Ya`akov. (26) They shall dwell securely therein; yes, they shall build houses, and plant vineyards, and shall dwell securely, when I have executed judgments on all those who do them despite round about them; and they shall know that I am the LORD their God.

Ezekiel 39:27-29 HNV when I have brought them back from the peoples, and gathered them out of their enemies' lands, and am sanctified in them in the sight of many nations. (28) They shall know that I am the LORD their God, in that I caused them to go into captivity among the nations, and have gathered them to their own land; and I will leave none of them any more there; (29) neither will I hide my face any more from them; for I have poured out my Spirit on the house of Yisra'el, says the Lord GOD.

Hosea 1:10-11 HNV Yet the number of the children of Yisra'el will be as the sand of the sea, which can't be measured nor numbered; and it will come to pass that, in the place where it was said to them, 'You are not my people,' they will be called 'sons of the living God.' (11) The children of Yehudah and the children of Yisra'el will be gathered together, and they will appoint themselves one head, and will go up from the land; for great will be the day of Yizre`el.

Zephaniah 3:14-20 HNV Sing, daughter of Tziyon! Shout, Yisra'el! Be glad and rejoice with all your heart, daughter of Yerushalayim. (15) The LORD has taken away your judgments. He has thrown out your enemy. The King of Yisra'el, the LORD, is in the midst of you. You will not be afraid of evil any more. (16) In that day, it will be said to Yerushalayim, "Don't be afraid, Tziyon. Don't let your hands be slack." (17) The LORD, your God, is in the midst of you, a mighty one who will save. He will rejoice over you with joy. He will rest in his love. He will rejoice over you with singing. (18) Those who are sad for the appointed feasts, I will remove from you. They are a burden and a reproach to you. (19) Behold, at that time I will deal with all those who afflict you, and I will save those who are lame, and gather those who were driven away. I will give them praise and honor, whose shame has been in all the earth. (20) At that time will I bring you in, and at that time will I gather you; for I will give you honor and praise among all the peoples of the earth, when I bring back your captivity before your eyes, says the LORD.

Matthew 12:30 HNV "He who is not with me is against me, and he who doesn't gather with me, scatters.

Matthew 23:37-39 HNV "Yerushalayim, Yerushalayim, who kills the prophets, and stones those who are sent to her! How often I would have gathered your children together, even as a hen gathers her chicks under her wings, and you would not! (38) Behold, your house is left to you desolate. (39) For I tell you, you will not see me from now on, until you say, 'Blessed is he who comes in the name of the Lord!'"

Ezekiel 36:25 is the next portion we will need to break down. It has to do with cleansing.

- I will sprinkle clean water on you,
- and you shall be clean:
- from all your filthiness,
- and from all your idols, will I cleanse you.

There is only one place that you will find the sprinkling of water explained and defined in Scripture; the book of Numbers chapter nineteen. This passage of scripture tells us what had to be done for a person who had touched the realm of death or any dead or unclean thing, in order for them to become cleansed. This is also a Messianic prophecy.

Numbers 19:1-2 HNV The LORD spoke to Moshe and to Aharon, saying, (2) This is the statute of the law which the LORD has commanded, saying, Speak to the children of Yisra'el, that they bring you a red heifer without spot, in which is no blemish, [and] on which never came yoke.

There is a shadow of our Messiah in the offering of the red heifer. He had to be perfect, spotless, blameless, with no defects and He had to have never known the yoke of sin. As His children, when He cleanses us, we will become as He is and we will be able to walk as He walked.

Job 11:12-15 HNV An empty-headed man becomes wise when a man is born as a wild donkey's colt. (13) "If you set your heart aright, stretch out your hands toward him. (14) If iniquity is in your hand, put it far away. Don't let unrighteousness dwell in your tents. (15) Surely then shall you lift up your face without spot; Yes, you shall be steadfast, and shall not fear:

1 Timothy 6:13-14 HNV I charge you before God, who gives life to all things, and before Messiah Yeshua, who before Pontius Pilate testified the good confession, (14) that you keep the mitzvah without spot, blameless, until the appearing of our Lord Yeshua the Messiah;

Hebrews 9:13-14 HNV For if the blood of goats and bulls, and the ashes of a heifer sprinkling those who have been defiled, sanctify to the cleanness of the flesh: (14) how much more will the blood of Messiah, who through the eternal Spirit offered himself without blemish to God, cleanse your conscience from dead works to serve the living God?

1 Peter 1:18-19 HNV knowing that you were redeemed, not with corruptible things, with silver or gold, from the useless way of life handed down from your fathers, (19) but with precious blood, as of a faultless and pure lamb, the blood of Messiah;

2 Peter 3:14 HNV Therefore, beloved, seeing that you look for these things, be diligent to be found in shalom, without blemish and blameless in his sight.

Ephesians 5:25-27 KJV Husbands, love your wives, even as Christ also loved the church, and gave himself for it; (26) That he might sanctify and cleanse it with the washing of water by the word, (27) That he might present it to himself a glorious church, not having spot, or wrinkle, or any such thing; but that it should be holy and without blemish.

Now without spot and blemish we are free from the yoke of sin and death!

Isaiah 10:27 HNV It will happen in that day, that his burden will depart from off your shoulder, and his yoke from off your neck, and the yoke shall be destroyed because of the anointing oil.

Nahum 1:12-13 HNV Thus says the LORD: "Though they be in full strength, and likewise many, even so they will be cut down, and he shall pass away. Though I have afflicted you, I will afflict you no more. (13) Now will I break his yoke from off you, and will burst your bonds apart."

Matthew 11:28-30 HNV "Come to me, all you who labor and are heavily burdened, and I will give you rest. (29) Take my yoke upon you, and learn from me, for I am gentle and lowly in heart; and you will find rest for your souls. (30) For my yoke is easy, and my burden is light."

The sprinkling of the water mixed with the ashes from the red heifer was to make one ceremonially clean. The paradox was, if it was to make someone clean, why did they have to be clean before they could prepare it? Why did all those involved in the cleansing process become unclean?

Numbers 19:7-10 HNV Then the Kohen shall wash his clothes, and he shall bathe his flesh in water, and afterward he shall come into the camp, and the *Kohen shall be unclean until the even*. (8) He who burns her shall wash his clothes in water, and bathe his flesh in water, *and shall be unclean until the even*. (9) A man who is clean shall gather up the ashes of the heifer, and lay them up outside of the camp in a clean place; and it shall be kept for the congregation of the children of Yisra'el for a water for impurity: it is a sin offering. (10) He who gathers the ashes of the heifer shall wash his clothes, *and be unclean until the even*: and it shall be to the children of Yisra'el, and to the stranger who lives as a foreigner among them, for a statute forever.

Job 14:4 KJV Who can bring a clean [thing] out of an unclean? not one.

2 Corinthians 5:21 HNV For him who knew no sin he made to be sin on our behalf; so that in him we might become the righteousness of God.

Like I said, these are shadows of the Messiah. The purpose was to cleanse you (to be ritually clean so that you could present an offering to the LORD), and to purify you.

Numbers 19:13 HNV Whoever touches a dead person, the body of a man who has died, and doesn't purify himself, defiles the tent of the LORD; and that soul shall be cut off from Yisra'el: because the water for impurity was not sprinkled on him, he shall be unclean; his uncleanness is yet on him.

Numbers 19:20 HNV But the man who shall be unclean, and shall not purify himself, that soul shall be cut off from the midst of the assembly, because he has defiled the sanctuary of the LORD: the water for impurity has not been sprinkled on him; he is unclean.

Zechariah 13:1 HNV "In that day there will be a spring opened to the house of David and to the inhabitants of Yerushalayim, for sin and for uncleanness. *(for purification)*

1 Corinthians 3:16-17 KJV Know ye not that ye are the temple of God, and *that* the Spirit of God dwelleth in you? (17) If any man defile the temple of God, him shall God destroy; for the temple of God is holy, which *temple* ye are.

Ezekiel 36:26 and the first part of 27 is what we will look at next.

- A new heart also will I give you,
- and a new spirit will I put within you;
- and I will take away the stony heart out of your flesh,
- and I will give you a heart of flesh.
- (27) HNV I will put my Spirit within you,

This really is amazing! We are told that we will receive a new heart. This was said earlier in Ezekiel 11 as well.

Ezekiel 11:18-19 HNV They shall come there, and they shall take away all the detestable things of it and all the abominations of it from there. (19) I will give them one heart, and I will put a new spirit within you; and I will take the stony heart out of their flesh, and will give them a heart of flesh;

The implication of these verses are amazing! A new heart that will be in complete unity? The only way we can be in complete unity is if we are united with the will of the Father. There are only two places in scripture where it was recorded that all were in unity. The first was when the Torah was given, the second was when the Ruach HaKodesh (Holy Spirit) was sent on Shavuot (what we call Pentecost).

Exodus 19:1-8 HNV In the third month after the children of Yisra'el had gone forth out of the land of Egypt, on that same day they came into the wilderness of Sinai. (2) When they had departed from Refidim, and had come to the wilderness of Sinai, they encamped in the wilderness; and there Yisra'el encamped before the mountain. (3) Moshe went up to God, and the LORD called to him out of the mountain, saying, "This is what you shall tell the house of Ya`akov, and tell the children of Yisra'el: (4) 'You have seen what I did to the Egyptians, and how I bore you on eagles' wings, and brought you to myself. (5) Now therefore, if you will indeed obey my voice, and keep my covenant, then you shall be my own possession from among all peoples; for all the earth is mine; (6) and you shall be to me a kingdom of Kohanim, and a holy nation.' These are the words which you shall speak to the children of Yisra'el." (7) Moshe came and called for the elders of the people, and set before them all these words which the LORD commanded him. (8) All the people answered together, and said,
- ***"All that the LORD has spoken***
- ***we will do."***
- Moshe reported the words of the people to the LORD.

Acts 2:1-6 KJV And when the day of Pentecost was fully come, they were all with one accord in one place. (2) And suddenly there came a sound from heaven as of a rushing mighty wind, and it filled all the house where they were sitting. (3) And there appeared unto them cloven tongues like as of fire, and it sat upon each of them. (4) And they were all filled with the Holy Ghost, and began to speak with other tongues, as the Spirit gave them utterance. (5) And there were dwelling at Jerusalem Jews, devout men, out of every nation under heaven. (6) Now when this was noised abroad, the multitude came together, and were confounded, because that every man heard them speak in his own language.

When we are in unity with the Father, we have had heart surgery. We receive into us His heart! Along with that, we receive the power to overcome the ways of this world, to walk in the ways, which is the word, of YHWH. We will no longer approach the word of the Father with a stony heart. It was our old sin natured heart that could not read and understand the word because we did not have the knowledge of the Messiah. When we have a heart unwilling to receive the word of the Father, we are placing a veil over our heart. The result will be a hardened heart. When we come to Him He will take the veil away, thereby removing our veiled hard heart. He will replace it with a new, unveiled heart, soft and tender for the word of the Father.

2 Corinthians 3:14-18 HNV But _their minds were hardened_, for until this very day at the reading of the old covenant the same **_veil_** remains, because _in Messiah It **(the veil)** passes away_. (15) But to this day, when Moshe is read, a **_veil_** lies on their heart. (16) But whenever one turns to the Lord, **_the veil is taken away_**. (17) Now the Lord is the Spirit and where the Spirit of the Lord is, there is liberty. (18) But we all, with **_unveiled face_** beholding as in a mirror the glory of the Lord, are transformed into the same image from glory to glory, even as from the Lord, the Spirit.

We now approach the word in the way it was given to us, as instructions for a better way. Couldn't we use a better way in our life? Remember as earlier discussed, this passage deals specifically with what Moses wrote. As we come to the Father, the veil will be removed to see the word fully. Too often we give our heart to the Father, but we want to keep the veil.

The next thing we see is that He will put His Spirit inside of us. I don't know about you, but I need His Spirit inside of me to lead and guide me through the word as I live my day to day life. We often hear that the Spirit of God moved _upon_ people of the Old Testament and moves _within_ new testament believers. God is God and does what He desires. You will see where He filled people with His Spirit, _even in the Torah._

It was testified of Joseph that the Spirit of God was **_in_** him.

Genesis 41:38-42 HNV Par`oh said to his servants, "Can we find such a one as this, a man **_in whom is the Spirit of God_**?" (39) Par`oh said to Yosef, "Because _God has shown you_ all of this, _there is none so discreet and wise_ (**_discerning_**) as you. (40) You shall be over my house, and according to your word will all my people be ruled. Only in the throne I will be greater than you." (41) Par`oh said to Yosef, "Behold, I have set you over all the land of Egypt." (42) Par`oh took off his signet ring from his hand, and put it on Yosef's hand, and arrayed him in robes of fine linen, and put a gold chain about his neck,

Notice why Pharaoh, the king of Egypt, declared that the Spirit of God was _in_ Joseph. It was because of his discernment and wisdom. This is important to remember as we move forward.

Peter made a statement in his writings that the prophets had the Spirit of God in them.

1 Peter 1:10-12 HNV Concerning this salvation, the prophets sought and searched diligently, who prophesied of the grace that would come to you, (11) searching for who or what kind of time the _Spirit of Messiah, which was **in** them_, pointed to, when he predicted the sufferings of Messiah, and the glories that would follow them. (12) To them it was revealed, that not to themselves, but to you, they ministered these things, which now have been announced to you through those who preached the Good News to you by the Holy Spirit sent out from heaven; which things angels desire to look into.

    I next want to tell you of a man named Bezaleel. He was the foreman in charge of making the furniture in the tabernacle. This was a great and complicated task ahead of him. Moshe gave him the blueprints and he had to build it to exact specifications. There was no room for even the slightest error. I would not want to undertake a responsibility like this without the spirit of God working through me. That is exactly what the Father did for him.

Exodus 31:1-3 HNV The LORD spoke to Moshe, saying, (2) "Behold, I have called by name Betzal'el the son of Uri, the son of Chur, of the tribe of Yehudah: (3) and <u>I have filled him with the Spirit of God</u>, in <u>wisdom</u>, and in <u>understanding</u>, and in <u>knowledge</u>, and in all manner of workmanship,

In this verse we have the Father making the declaration that He put *within* the man He chose, His Spirit. The word He used was filled. It was testified that Bezaleel was a Spirit filled man! The Hebrew word for filled here is the word Male':

H4390 - מָלֵא מָלָא-mâlê' mâlâ'-*maw-lay', maw-law'*

A primitive root, to *fill* or (intransitively) *be full of,* in a wide application (literally and figuratively): - accomplish, confirm, + consecrate, be at an end, be expired, be fenced, fill, fulfil, (be, become, X draw, give in, go) fully (-ly, -ly set, tale), [over-] flow, fulness, furnish, gather (selves, together), presume, replenish, satisfy, set, space, take a [hand-] full, + have wholly.

Look at the phrasing used to describe what the Father said He put in Bezaleel. He says He put His Spirit in him and that means he has wisdom, understanding and knowledge.

The first witness of the Spirit of the Father in you is wisdom.

H2451 חָכְמָה-chokmâh -*khok-maw'*

From H2449; *wisdom* (in a good sense): - skillful, wisdom, wisely, wit.

The second witness of the Spirit is understanding. This involves more than being mentally capable. It has to do with discernment.

H8394 - תָּבֻן תְּבוּנָה תּוֹבֻנָה -tâbûn tebûnâh tôbûnâh

taw-boon', teb-oo-naw', to-boo-naw'

The second and third forms being feminine; from H995; *intelligence*; by implication an *argument*; by extension *caprice*: - <u>discretion</u>, <u>reason</u>, <u>skilfulness</u>, <u>understanding</u>, <u>wisdom</u>.

From the word – **H995**- בִּין -bîyn *-bene*

A primitive root; <u>to separate mentally</u> (or *distinguish*), that is, (generally) <u>understand</u>: - attend, consider, be cunning, diligently, direct, <u>discern</u>, eloquent, feel, inform, <u>instruct</u>, have intelligence, know, look well to, mark, perceive, be prudent, regard, (can) skill (-ful), teach, think, (cause, make to, get, give, have) understand (-ing), view, (deal) wise (-ly, man).

The last witness we will list is Knowledge.

H1847 – דַּעַת -da'ath *-dah'-ath*

From H3045; *knowledge*: - cunning, [ig-] norantly, know(-ledge), [un-] awares (wittingly).

From the word, that means an intimate knowing. Like a husband would know a wife. This is more than knowing about someone, this is knowing them!

H3045 – יָדַע -yâda' *-yaw-dah'*

A primitive root; <u>to know</u> (properly <u>to ascertain by seeing</u>); used in a great variety of senses, figuratively, literally, euphemistically and inferentially (including *observation, care, recognition*; and causatively *instruction, designation, punishment*, etc.): - acknowledge, acquaintance (-ted with), advise, answer, appoint, assuredly, be aware, [un-] awares, can [-not], certainly, for a certainty, <u>comprehend</u>, consider, X could they, cunning, declare, be diligent, (can, cause to) <u>discern</u>, <u>discover</u>, endued with, <u>familiar friend,</u> famous, feel, can have, be [ig-] norant, instruct, kinsfolk, kinsman, (cause to, let, make) know, (come to give, have, take) knowledge, have [knowledge], (be, make, make to be, make self) known, + be learned, + lie by man, mark, perceive, privy to, X prognosticator, regard, *have respect*, *skilfu*l, shew, can (man of) skill, be sure, of a surety, teach, (can) tell, *understand*, have [understanding], X will be, wist, wit, wot.

    I have people get upset with me all of the time because I say that it doesn't matter to me how much scripture they know and can quote. I am <u>not</u> saying not to study! I am saying, get it out of your head and into your heart so it can produce the fruit in your life that it is intended to. I would much rather someone have a solid grasp on the word they do know by applying it, than just trying to impress someone with knowledge.

    We will never grow up and mature in the Body of Messiah as long as we are trying to out-quote and out-teach one another. We need to apply the word to our hearts and let it be written by the Spirit. It's time to stop comparing ourselves to each other and to let the Father do the work in us that He has planned for us.

2 Corinthians 10:12 HNV For we are not bold to number or compare ourselves with some of those who commend themselves. But they themselves, measuring themselves by themselves, and comparing themselves with themselves, are without understanding.

    In the following verses you will see that the testimony of the Spirit of YHWH being in you goes hand in hand with having wisdom, understanding and knowledge. Remember what knowledge means. I am not referring to how much you know or how many facts or verses you can quote. I am speaking of an intimate knowing with the One who created you.

Deuteronomy 4:5-6 HNV Behold, I have taught you statutes and ordinances, even as the LORD my God commanded me, that you should do so in the midst of the land where you go in to possess it. (6) Keep therefore and do them; for _this is your wisdom and your understanding_ in the sight of the peoples, who shall hear all these statutes, and say, Surely this great nation is a wise and understanding people.

Our witness, and testimony, that we walk in the word, is that we have wisdom and understanding. It was testified that Joshua was full of wisdom and the Spirit.

Deuteronomy 34:9 HNV Yehoshua the son of Nun was _full of the spirit of wisdom_; for Moshe had laid his hands on him: and the children of Yisra'el listened to him, and did as the LORD commanded Moshe.

Proverbs 1:1-5 HNV The proverbs of Shlomo, the son of David, king of Yisra'el: (2) to know _wisdom and instruction_; to _discern the words of understanding_; (3) to receive instruction in _wise dealing_, in righteousness, justice, and equity; (4) to give prudence to the simple, _knowledge and discretion_ to the young man: (5) that the wise man may hear, and increase in learning; that the man of understanding may attain to sound counsel:

Proverbs 2:5-6 HNV then you will understand the fear of the LORD, and find the knowledge of God. (6) For the LORD gives wisdom. Out of his mouth comes knowledge and understanding.

Proverbs 9:10 HNV The fear of the LORD is the beginning of wisdom. The knowledge of the Holy One is understanding.

Proverbs 14:6 HNV A scoffer seeks wisdom, and doesn't find it, but knowledge comes easily to a discerning person.

Proverbs 15:14 HNV   The heart of one who has understanding seeks knowledge, but the mouths of fools feed on folly.

Colossians 1:7-10 HNV even as you learned of Epaphras our beloved fellow servant, who is a faithful servant of Messiah on our behalf, (8) who also declared to us your love in the

Spirit. (9) For this cause, we also, since the day we heard this, don't cease praying and making requests for you, that you may be filled with the knowledge of his will in all spiritual wisdom and understanding, (10) that you may walk worthily of the Lord, to please him in all respects, bearing fruit in every good work, and increasing in the knowledge of God;
Colossians 2:2-4 HNV that their hearts may be comforted, they being knit together in love, and gaining all riches of the full assurance of understanding, that they may know the mystery of God, both of the Father and of Messiah, (3) in whom are all the treasures of wisdom and knowledge hidden. (4) Now this I say that no one may delude you with persuasiveness of speech.

Philemon 1:6 HNV that the fellowship of your faith may become effective, in the knowledge of every good thing which is in us in Messiah Yeshua.

James 3:13-18 HNV Who is wise and understanding among you? Let him show by his good conduct that his deeds are done in gentleness of wisdom. (14) But if you have bitter jealousy and selfish ambition in your heart, don't boast and don't lie against the truth. (15) This wisdom is not that which comes down from above, but is earthly, sensual, and demonic. (16) For where jealousy and selfish ambition are, there is confusion and every evil deed. (17) But the wisdom that is from above is first pure, then peaceful, gentle, reasonable, full of mercy and good fruits, without partiality, and without hypocrisy. (18) Now the fruit of righteousness is sown in peace by those who make shalom.

1 Corinthians 2:12-16 HNV But we received, not the spirit of the world, but the Spirit which is from God, that we might know the things that were freely given to us by God. (13) Which things also we speak, not in words which man's wisdom teaches, but which the Holy Spirit teaches, comparing spiritual things with spiritual things. (14) Now the natural man doesn't receive the things of God's Spirit, for they are foolishness to him, and he can't know them, because they are spiritually discerned. (15) But he who is spiritual discerns all things, and he himself is judged by no one. (16)

"For who has known the mind of the Lord, that he should instruct him?" But we have Messiah's mind.

1 Kings 3:6-14 HNV Shlomo said, You have shown to your servant David my father great loving kindness, according as he walked before you in truth, and in righteousness, and in uprightness of heart with you; and you have kept for him this great loving kindness, that you have given him a son to sit on his throne, as it is this day. (7) Now, LORD my God, you have made your servant king instead of David my father: and I am but a little child; I don't know how to go out or come in. (8) Your servant is in the midst of your people which you have chosen, a great people, that can't be numbered nor counted for multitude. (9) Give your servant therefore an understanding heart to judge your people, that I may discern between good and evil; for who is able to judge this your great people? (10) The speech pleased the Lord, that Shlomo had asked this thing. (11) God said to him, Because you have asked this thing, and have not asked for yourself long life, neither have asked riches for yourself, nor have asked the life of your enemies, but have asked for yourself understanding to discern justice; (12) behold, I have done according to your word: behold, I have given you a wise and an understanding heart; so that there has been none like you before you, neither after you shall any arise like you. (13) I have also given you that which you have not asked, both riches and honor, so that there shall not be any among the kings like you, all your days. (14) If you will walk in my ways, to keep my statutes and my mitzvot, as your father David did walk, then I will lengthen your days.

Isaiah 40:13-14 HNV Who has directed the Spirit of the LORD, or has taught him as his counselor? (14) Who did he take counsel with, and who instructed him, and taught him in the path of justice, and taught him knowledge, and showed him the way of understanding?

Daniel 12:2-4 HNV Many of those who sleep in the dust of the earth shall awake, some to everlasting life, and some to shame and everlasting contempt. (3) Those who are wise shall shine as the brightness of the expanse; and those who turn many to righteousness as the stars forever and ever. (4)

But you, Daniyel, shut up the words, and seal the book, even to the time of the end: many shall run back and forth, and knowledge shall be increased."

The last part of Ezekiel 36 we need to look at is verse twenty seven.

Ezekiel 36:27 I will put my Spirit inside you
- and cause you
- to walk in my statutes,
- and you shall keep my ordinances,
- and do them.

Once we are drawn and brought back home, we get a heart transplant. After the new heart, we receive the Spirit of the living God. The purpose of the Spirit of YHWH is to draw us closer to Him through His word. His Spirit will equip us to live according to the word we have been given. Look specifically at what it says, it will cause you to walk in His laws (Torah-teachings), rulings and obey them.

The word that is translated as law here is the Hebrew word "Choq"

H2706 –חק -chôq -khoke

From H2710; an *enactment*; hence an *appointment* (of time, space, quantity, labor or usage): - appointed, bound, commandment, convenient, custom, decree (-d), due, law, measure, X necessary, ordinance (-nary), portion, set time, statute, task.

The word choq means appointment, commandment, custom or decree. These are the things in scripture that the rabbis explain by saying "Because God said so". These do not make sense to us, we do them out of sheer obedience.

Exodus 15:26 HNV and he said, "If you will diligently listen to the voice of the LORD your God, and will do that which is right in his eyes, and will pay attention to his mitzvot, and keep all his statutes, I will put none of the diseases on you, which I have put on the Egyptians; for I am the LORD who heals you."

Deuteronomy 6:20-25 HNV When your son asks you in time to come, saying, What mean the testimonies, and the statutes, and the ordinances, which the LORD our God has commanded you? (21) then you shall tell your son, We were Par`oh's bondservants in Egypt: and the LORD brought us out of Egypt with a mighty hand; (22) and the LORD showed great and awesome signs and wonders on Egypt, on Par`oh, and on all his house, before our eyes; (23) and he brought us out from there, that he might bring us in, to give us the land which he swore to our fathers. (24) The LORD commanded us to do all these statutes, to fear the LORD our God, for our good always, that he might preserve us alive, as at this day. (25) It shall be righteousness to us, if we observe to do all this mitzvah before the LORD our God, as he has commanded us.

Deuteronomy 5:1-7 HNV Moshe called to all Yisra'el, and said to them, Hear, Yisra'el, the statutes and the ordinances which I speak in your ears this day, that you may learn them, and observe to do them. (2) The LORD our God made a covenant with us in Chorev. (3) The LORD didn't make this covenant with our fathers, but with us, even us, who are all of us here alive this day. (4) The LORD spoke with you face to face on the mountain out of the midst of the fire, (5) (I stood between the LORD and you at that time, to show you the word of the LORD: for you were afraid because of the fire, and didn't go up onto the mountain;) saying, (6) "I am the LORD your God, who brought you out of the land of Egypt, out of the house of bondage. (7) You shall have no other gods before me.

We are to keep the word of YHWH. To keep here means to protect and attend to, to preserve, to hedge around with thorns! How many of you have prayed like that. It's not a new testament concept. It originated as an aspect of guarding and protecting the things of YHWH. The word used for "respect" or "keep" in Ezekiel 36:27 is the Hebrew word "Shamar".

H8104- שָׁמַר   -shâmar-*shaw-mar'*

A primitive root; properly to *hedge* about (as with thorns), that is, *guard*; generally to *protect, attend to*, etc.: - beware, be circumspect, take heed (to self), keep (-er, self), mark, look narrowly, observe, preserve, regard, reserve, save (self), sure, (that lay) wait (for), watch (-man).

So we are to keep, guard and protect something. What is it? The last word we will look at in this passage is "judgments".

H4941-מִשְׁפָּט   -mishpâṭ-*mish-pawt'*

From H8199; properly <u>a verdict</u> (favorable or unfavorable) pronounced judicially, especially <u>a sentence or formal decree</u> (human or (particularly) divine *law*, individual or collectively), including the act, the place, the suit, the crime, and the penalty; abstractly *justice*, including a <u>particular right, or privilege</u> (statutory or customary), or even a *style:* - + adversary, ceremony, charge, X crime, <u>custom</u>, desert, determination, discretion, disposing, due, fashion, form, to be judged, <u>judgment, just (-ice, -ly),</u> (manner of) law (-ful), <u>manner</u>, measure, (due) order, ordinance, right, sentence, usest, X worthy, + wrong.

    The word mishpat could easily be translated as judgment. We don't like to hear this word. For the believer, judgment is not a bad or negative thing. The flood that was sent in Noah's day was a judgment. Who was spared from the flood? Noah and his family were judged with the inhabitants of the earth and were found faithful. They were spared.

    When Israel was in slavery in the land of Egypt, Egypt was judged. Israel came out favorably in the judgment. As a matter of fact, the Father said that He would put a distinction between the ones who belonged to Him and Egypt.

1 Kings 8:53 HNV For you did separate them from among all the peoples of the earth, to be your inheritance, as you spoke by Moshe your servant, when you brought our fathers out of Egypt, Lord GOD.

Exodus 8:22-23 HNV I will set apart in that day the land of Goshen, in which my people dwell, that no swarms of flies shall be there; to the end you may know that I am the LORD in the midst of the earth. (23) I will put a division between my people and your people: by tomorrow shall this sign be.""''

Exodus 9:3-5 HNV behold, the hand of the LORD is on your livestock which are in the field, on the horses, on the donkeys, on the camels, on the herds, and on the flocks with a very grievous pestilence. (4) The LORD will make a distinction between the livestock of Yisra'el and the livestock of Egypt; and there shall nothing die of all that belongs to the children of Yisra'el.""'' (5) The LORD appointed a set time, saying, "Tomorrow the LORD shall do this thing in the land."

    The Father makes a distinction between His people and He does it by His mishpat, (judgment). The breastplate that Aaron wore, that had the names of the tribes on it, was called the breastplate of judgment. If we are to come to the Father and walk in His Spirit and be refreshed in it, we need to understand His righteous judgment.

Proverbs 28:4-5 HNV Those who forsake the law praise the wicked; but those who keep the law contend with them. (5) Evil men don't understand justice; but those who seek the LORD understand it fully.

Proverbs 28:4-5   Those who abandon Torah praise the wicked, but those who keep Torah fight them. (5) Evil people don't understand justice *(mishpat – justice or judgment)* but those who seek Adonai understand everything.

To walk in the Spirit means to walk according to the word. In order to walk in the Word you need the Spirit, which gives wisdom, understanding and knowledge. When you walk in these, it will be refreshing for you. You will be equipped to walk in the path that leads to life and was given from the heart of the Father.

When we walk in His ways, we not only will be refreshed, but we will be refreshing to others. We will become a river!

NOTES

NOTES

Chapter Seven

THE RIVER OF REFRESHING

Psalms 1:1-6 HNV Blessed is the man who doesn't walk in the counsel of the wicked, nor stand in the way of sinners, nor sit in the seat of scoffers; (2) but his delight is in the LORD's law (*Torah- teaching*). On his law he meditates day and night. (3) He will be like a tree planted by the streams of water, that brings forth its fruit in its season, whose leaf also does not wither. Whatever he does shall prosper. (4) The wicked are not so, but are like the chaff which the wind drives away. (5) Therefore the wicked shall not stand in the judgment, nor sinners in the congregation of the righteous. (6) For the LORD knows the way of the righteous, but the way of the wicked shall perish.

Look at verse three above, a righteous man will be like a tree planted by streams, bearing fruit at the right season, and his leaves do not whither. What we will come to see is that not only is he the tree, he is the water as well. I know, the water represents Yeshua as the living water. You are correct. But it doesn't stop there.

To look at this a little deeper, we will start by looking at Ezekiel's temple and the river that flows through it.

Ezekiel 47:1-12 HNV He brought me back to the door of the house; and behold, waters issued out from under the threshold of the house eastward; (for the forefront of the house was toward the east;) and the waters came down from under, from the right side of the house, on the south of the altar. (2) Then he brought me out by the way of the gate northward, and led me round by the way outside to the outer gate, by the way of [the gate] that looks toward the east; and behold, there ran out waters on the right side. (3) When the man went forth eastward with the line in his hand, he measured one thousand cubits, and he caused me to pass through the waters, waters that were to the ankles. (4) Again he measured one thousand, and caused me to pass through the waters, waters that were to the knees. Again he measured one thousand, and caused me to pass through [the waters], waters that were to the waist. (5) Afterward he measured one thousand; [and it was] a river that I could not pass through; for the waters were risen, waters to swim in, a river that could not be passed through. (6) He said to me, Son of man, have you seen [this]? Then he brought me, and caused me to return to the bank of the river. (7) Now when I had returned, behold, on the bank of the river were very many trees on the one side and on the other. (8) Then said he to me, These waters issue forth toward the eastern region, and shall go down into the `Aravah; and they shall go toward the sea; into the sea [shall the waters go] which were made to issue forth; and the waters shall be healed. (9) It shall happen, that every living creature which swarms, in every place where the rivers come, shall live; and there shall be a very great multitude of fish; for these waters are come there, and [the waters of the sea] shall be healed, and everything shall live wherever the river comes. (10) It shall happen, that fishermen shall stand by it: from `En-Gedi even to `En-`Eglayim shall be a place for the spreading of nets; their fish shall be after their kinds, as the fish of the great sea, exceeding many. (11) But the miry places of it, and the marshes of it, shall not be healed; they shall be given up to salt.

- (12) By the river on the bank of it,
- on this side and on that side,
- shall grow every tree for food,
- whose leaf shall not wither,
- neither shall the fruit of it fail:
- it shall bring forth new fruit every month,
- because the <u>*waters of it issue out of the sanctuary*</u>;
- and the fruit of it shall be for food,
- and the leaf of it for healing.

It is interesting to note that the eastern gate of the temple was also called the water gate. That was where the food offerings that belonged to the priests were distributed.

2 Chronicles 31:14 HNV Kore the son of Yimna the Levite, the porter at the east [gate], was over the freewill offerings of

God, to distribute the offerings of the LORD, and the most holy things.

Nehemiah 3:25-26 HNV Palal the son of Uzai [repaired] over against the turning [of the wall], and the tower that stands out from the upper house of the king, which is by the court of the guard. After him Pedayahu the son of Par`osh [repaired]. (26) (Now the temple servants 1 lived in `Ofel, to the place over against the water gate toward the east, and the tower that stands out.)

Nehemiah 12:37 HNV By the spring gate, and straight before them, they went up by the stairs of the city of David, at the ascent of the wall, above the house of David, even to the water gate eastward.

We see that there was a lot that happened at the east gate. The Father also revealed His glory at the east gate. The glory of the Father was shown at the gate where His food was distributed! Think back to what Yeshua said about not living on bread alone but by every word from the mouth of YHWH.

Ezekiel 43:1-9 HNV Afterward he brought me to the gate, even the gate that looks toward the east. (2) Behold, the glory of the God of Yisra'el came from the way of the east: and his voice was like the sound of many waters; and the earth shined with his glory. (3) It was according to the appearance of the vision which I saw, even according to the vision that I saw when I came to destroy the city; and the visions were like the vision that I saw by the river Kevar; and I fell on my face. (4) The glory of the LORD came into the house by the way of the gate whose prospect is toward the east. (5) The Spirit took me up, and brought me into the inner court; and behold, the glory of the LORD filled the house. (6) I heard one speaking to me out of the house; and a man stood by me. (7) He said to me, Son of man, [this is] the place of my throne, and the place of the soles of my feet, where I will dwell in the midst of the children of Yisra'el forever. The house of Yisra'el shall no more defile my holy name, neither they, nor their kings, by their prostitution, and by the dead bodies of their kings [in] their high places; (8) in their setting of their threshold by my threshold, and their doorpost beside my doorpost, and there was [but] the wall between me and them; and they have defiled my holy name by their abominations which they have committed: therefore I have consumed them in my anger. (9) Now let them put away their prostitution, and the dead bodies of their kings, far from me; and I will dwell in the midst of them forever.

Ezekiel 44:1-3 HNV Then he brought me back by the way of the outer gate of the sanctuary, which looks toward the east; and it was shut. (2) The LORD said to me, This gate shall be shut; it shall not be opened, neither shall any man enter in by it; for the LORD, the God of Yisra'el, has entered in by it; therefore it shall be shut. (3) As for the prince, he shall sit therein as prince to eat bread before the LORD; he shall enter by the way of the porch of the gate, and shall go out by the way of the same.

This is awesome, YHWH went through the gate! After He came through the gate it was set aside to be used only for the prince, the Son of the King! A gate was also called a door. Yeshua said that He is the door!

John 10:1-9 HNV "Most certainly, I tell you, one who doesn't enter by the door into the sheep fold, but climbs up some other way, the same is a thief and a robber. (2) But one who enters in by the door is the shepherd of the sheep. (3) The gatekeeper opens the gate for him, and the sheep listen to his voice. He calls his own sheep by name, and leads them out. (4) Whenever he brings out his own sheep, he goes before them, and the sheep follow him, for they know his voice. (5) They will by no means follow a stranger, but will flee from him; for they don't know the voice of strangers." (6) Yeshua spoke this parable to them, but they didn't understand what he was telling them. (7) Yeshua therefore said to them again, "Most certainly, I tell you, I am the sheep's door. (8) All who came before me are thieves and robbers, but the sheep didn't listen to them. (9) I am the door. If anyone enters in by me, he will be saved, and will go in and go out, and will find pasture.

The east gate, the Water Gate, is where YHWH reveals His glory and that the Prince will sit and eat of the word of

YHWH. This is where the food was distributed, and where Yeshua (as the prince) will partake of the food. Combine all of this with knowing that we are invited to dine with Him. We can see ourselves in this illustration.

He is the door in which the Father chose to bring the sheep in and to bring praise to His name. This is amazing to look at in the Hebrew. The word for "door" or "gate" is Delet.

H1817

דֶּלֶת

deleth

deh'-leth

From H1802; something *swinging*, that is, the *valve* of a door: - door (two-leaved), gate, leaf, lid. [In Psa 141:3, *dal*, irreg.]

The name of the Father is made up of three Hebrew letters and four spaces it is YHWH.

H3068

יְהֹוָה

yᵉhôvâh

yeh-ho-vaw'

From H1961; (the) *self Existent* or eternal; *Jehovah*, Jewish national name of God: - Jehovah, the Lord. Compare H3050, H3069.

In order to give us a doorway to Him, He gave us His Son who is the Lion of the Tribe of Judah. Judah is the Hebrew "Yehudah".

H3063

יְהוּדָה

yᵉhûdâh

yeh-hoo-daw'

From H3034; *celebrated*; *Jehudah* (or Judah), the name of five Israelites; also of the tribe descended from the first, and of its territory: - Judah.

Look at the difference between the word "YHWH" and "Yehudah" the difference is the door. Who is the door? Yeshua is the door! Another way to look at this is praise directed toward the Father will bring us closer to Him. Look at the chart listing the difference between the two words.

יְהוָה	YHWH
דֶלֶת	Inserted the door- Delet
יְהוּדָה	To bring praise and celebration to His name- Yehudah

The east side of the Temple was supposed to be prepared for the glory of YHWH. Today at the east side of the temple mount is a Muslim graveyard. We have taken something that was supposed to be set apart and defiled it with the realm of death, or at the very least, something unclean.

Ezekiel 43:6-9 HNV I heard one speaking to me out of the house; and a man stood by me. (7) He said to me, Son of man, [this is] the place of my throne, and the place of the soles of my feet, where I will dwell in the midst of the children of Yisra'el forever. The house of Yisra'el shall no more defile my holy name, neither they, nor their kings, by their prostitution, and by the dead bodies of their kings [in] their high places; (8) in their setting of their threshold by my threshold, and their doorpost beside my doorpost, and there was [but] the wall between me and them; and they have defiled my holy name by their abominations which they have committed: therefore I have consumed them in my anger. (9) Now let them put away their prostitution, and the dead bodies of their kings, far from me; and I will dwell in the midst of them forever.

A flowing river will bring refreshing and cleansing wherever it flows. A flowing river is used to bring life and sustenance. It is to give water to the people so that they will have life! What do you call a river without banks that doesn't flow? A swamp. This river will wash away the uncleanness and bring life!

- The river from the temple will cleanse and purify anything it touches
- Where does this river flow from?
- The holy of holies!
- You!
- It will bring life where there was no life!

You were created, fashioned and formed to house the glory and Spirit of the living God! He desires to live in and through you!

1 Corinthians 6:19-20 HNV Or don't you know that your body is a temple of **_the Holy Spirit which is in you_**, which you have from God? You are not your own, (20) for you were bought with a price. Therefore glorify God in your body and in your spirit, which are God's.

Ezekiel 37:13-14 HNV You shall know that I am the LORD, when I have opened your graves, and caused you to come up out of your graves, my people. (14) **_I will put my Spirit in you_**, and you shall live, and I will place you in your own land: and you shall know that I, the LORD, have spoken it and performed it, says the LORD.

Daniel 4:4-9 HNV I, Nevukhadnetzar 1, was at rest in my house, and flourishing in my palace. (5) I saw a dream which made me afraid; and the thoughts on my bed and the visions of my head troubled me. (6) Therefore made I a decree to bring in all the wise men of Bavel before me, that they might make known to me the interpretation of the dream. (7) Then came in the magicians, the enchanters, the Kasdim, and the soothsayers; and I told the dream before them; but they did not make known to me the interpretation of it. (8) But at the last Daniyel came in before me, whose name was Belteshatzar, according to the name of my god, and in whom is the spirit of the holy gods: and I told the dream before him, [saying], (9) Belteshatzar, master of the magicians, because I know that the spirit of the holy gods is ***in you***, and no secret troubles you, tell me the visions of my dream that I have seen, and the interpretation of it.

Daniel 6:3 HNV Then this Daniyel was distinguished above the presidents and the satraps, because an excellent ***spirit was in him***; and the king thought to set him over the whole realm.

Haggai 2:4-5 HNV Yet now be strong, Zerubbavel,' says the LORD. 'Be strong, Yehoshua, son of Yehotzadak, the Kohen Gadol. Be strong, all you people of the land,' says the LORD, 'and work, for I am with you,' says the LORD of Armies. (5) This is the word that I covenanted with you when you came out of Egypt, ***and my Spirit lived among (within) you***. 'Don't be afraid.' –(parenthesis added)

Luke 4:1-2 HNV Yeshua, ***full of the Holy Spirit***, returned from the Yarden, and was led by the Spirit into the wilderness (2) for forty days, being tempted by the devil. He ate nothing in those days. Afterward, when they were completed, he was hungry.

1 Corinthians 3:16-17 HNV Don't you know that you are a temple of God, and that ***God's Spirit lives in you***? (17) If

anyone destroys the temple of God, God will destroy him; for God's temple is holy, which you are.

1 Peter 1:10-13 HNV Concerning this salvation, the prophets sought and searched diligently, who prophesied of the grace that would come to you, (11) searching for who or what kind of time **the Spirit of Messiah, which was in them**, pointed to, when he predicted the sufferings of Messiah, and the glories that would follow them. (12) To them it was revealed, that not to themselves, but to you, they ministered these things, which now have been announced to you through those who preached the Good News to you by the Holy Spirit sent out from heaven; which things angels desire to look into. (13) Therefore, prepare your minds for action, be sober and set your hope fully on the grace that will be brought to you at the revelation of Yeshua the Messiah--

When we come to the Father, He will give us His Spirit and dwell within us. He wants us to come to Him and be cleansed from all of our uncleanness and to wash our sin away. We will become a vessel to be used to house His glory. We will no longer be a people who have forsaken the Father and not held the Living water. We need to re-dig the wells of the forefathers of our faith, Abraham, Isaac and Jacob. We need to restore the living water to a dry and weary land.

Jeremiah 2:13 HNV For my people have committed two evils: they have forsaken me, the spring of living waters, and hewed them out cisterns, broken cisterns, that can hold no water.

Jeremiah 17:12-14 HNV   A glorious throne, [set] on high from the beginning, is the place of our sanctuary.   (13) LORD, the hope of Yisra'el, all who forsake you shall be disappointed. Those who depart from me shall be written in the earth, because they have forsaken the LORD, the spring of living waters. (14)   Heal me, O LORD, and I shall be healed; save me, and I shall be saved: for you are my praise.

Zechariah 14:8-9 HNV It will happen in that day, that living waters will go out from Yerushalayim; half of them toward the eastern sea, and half of them toward the western sea; in summer and in winter will it be. (9) The LORD will be King over all the earth. In that day the LORD will be one, and his name one.

- What do you think the living waters are?

- The water is listed as them not it!

- The water is you!

- You will carry in you, the living water!

John 4:10-14 HNV Yeshua answered her, "If you knew the gift of God, and who it is who says to you, 'Give me a drink,' you would have asked him, and he would have given you living water." (11) The woman said to him, "Sir, you have nothing to draw with, and the well is deep. From where then have you that living water? (12) Are you greater than our father, Ya`akov, who gave us the well, and drank of it himself, as did his children, and his livestock?" (13) Yeshua answered her, "Everyone who drinks of this water will thirst again, (14) but whoever drinks of the water that I will give him will never thirst again; but the water that I will give him will become in him a well of water springing up to eternal life."

- The One who is the living water

- Dwells in you

- He is creating inside of you a living spring!

John 7:38-39 KJV *He that believeth on me, as the scripture hath said, out of his belly shall flow rivers of living water.* (39) (But this spake he of the Spirit, which they that believe on him should receive: for the Holy Ghost was not yet *given;* because that Jesus was not yet glorified.)

- Yeshua said all that He had, He gave to you!

Matthew 28:18-20 KJV And Jesus came and spake unto them, saying, All power is given unto me in heaven and in earth. (19) Go ye therefore, and teach all nations, baptizing them in the name of the Father, and of the Son, and of the Holy Ghost: (20) Teaching them to observe all things whatsoever I have commanded you: and, lo, I am with you alway, [even] unto the end of the world. Amen.

John 17:6-8 HNV I revealed your name to the people whom you have given me out of the world. They were yours, and you have given them to me. They have kept your word. (7) Now they have known that all things whatever you have given me are from you, (8) for the words which you have given me I have given to them, and they received them, and knew for sure that I came forth from you, and they have believed that you sent me.

Romans 8:9-18 HNV But you are not in the flesh but in the Spirit, if it is so that the Spirit of God dwells in you. But if any man doesn't have the Spirit of Messiah, he is not his. (10) If Messiah is in you, the body is dead because of sin, but the spirit is alive because of righteousness. (11) But if the Spirit of him who raised up Yeshua from the dead dwells in you, he who raised up Messiah Yeshua from the dead will also give life to your mortal bodies through his Spirit who dwells in you. (12) So then, brothers, we are debtors, not to the flesh, to live after the flesh. (13) For if you live after the flesh, you must die; but if by the Spirit you put to death the deeds of the body, you will live. (14) For as many as are led by the Spirit of God, these are children of God. (15) For you didn't receive the spirit of bondage again to fear, but you received the Spirit of adoption, by whom we cry, "Abba! Father!" (16) The Spirit himself testifies with our spirit that we are children of God; (17) and if children, then heirs; heirs of God, and joint heirs with Messiah; if indeed we suffer with him, that we may also be glorified with him. (18) For I consider that the sufferings of this present time are not worthy to be compared with the glory which will be revealed toward us.

- He is the living water
- You are the living water
- What is living water used for?
- To cleanse
- To purify
- To heal
- To give life

If you are the living water, what are you giving? Is it;

- Cleansing
- Purification
- Healing
- Life!

What grew on the banks of the river?

Trees! Not just any trees, great trees that produced good fruit every month. There was new, fresh and good fruit every month of every season! This testifies of a consistent walk with the Father. The leaves of the trees were for healing, not just for you, but for the nations!

Revelation 22:1-2 HNV He showed me a river of water of life, clear as crystal, proceeding out of the throne of God and of the Lamb, (2) in the middle of its street. On this side of the river and on that was the tree of life, bearing twelve kinds of fruits, yielding its fruit every month. The leaves of the tree were for the healing of the nations.

Psalms 1:1-3 HNV Blessed is the man who doesn't walk in the counsel of the wicked, nor stand in the way of sinners, nor sit in the seat of scoffers; (2) but his delight is in the LORD's law. On his law he meditates day and night. (3) He will be like a tree planted by the streams of water, that brings forth its fruit in its season, whose leaf also does not wither. Whatever he does shall prosper.

How does a tree (a symbol of you) have good fruit and healthy leaves? You must have good roots and reject the advice of evil people. We may call that having discernment. It starts with reading and keeping the word we have been given.

We should find joy in doing (shema to hear and do) the word of YHWH. Lastly, you will need to have a good water supply and a good amount of light, which is Yeshua.

The leaves were for healing (***restoration***) of the nations (10 lost tribes, the lost sheep and all those who are grafted in).If the leaves have no water (life) in them, they cannot give life. Therefore they cannot give healing or restoration.

- ***A good tree has good, deep roots***

- Deep roots hold the tree solid and firm when storms and hurricanes come

- A good root system is constantly growing deeper and seeking nourishment

- A good tree provides fruit and shade for generations to come

Proverbs 13:22 HNV A good man leaves an inheritance to his children's children, but the wealth of the sinner is stored for the righteous.

Jeremiah 17:7-8 HNV Blessed is the man who trusts in the LORD, and whose trust the LORD is. (8) For he shall be as a tree planted by the waters, who spreads out its roots by the river, and shall not fear when heat comes, but its leaf shall be green; and shall not be careful in the year of drought, neither shall cease from yielding fruit.

- What was in the river?
- Life (Messiah)
- Fish (a picture of you)
- Fishermen (those who helped us cross over the river, and now you helping others)
- Ezekiel (man of God)
- You

Jeremiah 16:15-19 HNV but, As the LORD lives, who brought up the children of Yisra'el from the land of the north, and from all the countries where he had driven them. I will bring them again into their land that I gave to their fathers. (16) Behold, I will send for many fishermen, says the LORD, and they shall fish them up; and afterward I will send for many hunters, and they shall hunt them from every mountain, and from every hill, and out of the clefts of the rocks. (17) For my eyes are on all their ways; they are not hidden from my face, neither is their iniquity concealed from my eyes. (18) First I will recompense their iniquity and their sin double, because they have polluted my land with the carcasses of their detestable things, and have filled my inheritance with their abominations. (19) LORD, my strength, and my stronghold, and my refuge in the day of affliction, to you shall the nations come from the ends of the earth, and shall say, Our fathers have inherited nothing but lies, [even] vanity and things in which there is no profit.

Matthew 4:14-19 CJB This happened in order to fulfill what Yesha`yahu (Isaiah) the prophet had said, (15) "Land of Z'vulun and land of Naftali, toward the lake, beyond the Yarden, Galil-of-the-Goyim (16) the people living in darkness have seen a great light; upon those living in the region, in the shadow of death, light has dawned." (17) From that time on, Yeshua began proclaiming, "Turn from your sins to God, for the Kingdom of Heaven is near!" (18) As Yeshua walked by Lake Kinneret, he saw two brothers who were fishermen -- Shim`on, known as Kefa, and his brother Andrew -- throwing their net into the lake. (19) Yeshua said to them, "Come after me, and I will make you fishers for men!"

Isaiah 9:1-2 HNV But there shall be no more gloom for her who was in anguish. In the former time, he brought into contempt the land of Zevulun and the land of Naftali; but in the latter time he has made it glorious, by the way of the sea, beyond the Yarden, Galil of the nations. (2) The people who walked in darkness have seen a great light. Those who lived in the land of the shadow of death, on them the light has shined.

Though you live in a land all around of death and shadows...

Be that light before men! The same light Yeshua was, He called you to be!

Revelation 22:1-4 HNV He showed me a ***river of water of life***, clear as crystal, proceeding out of the throne of God and of the Lamb, (2) in the middle of its street. On this side of the river and on that was the tree of life, bearing twelve kinds of fruits, yielding its fruit every month. The leaves of the tree were for the healing of the nations. (3) There will be no curse any more. The throne of God and of the Lamb will be in it, and his servants serve him. (4) *They will see his face, and his name will be on their foreheads.*

    This is quite an interesting phrase. "His name shall be on their foreheads." Why didn't John just say that the Spirit of God was inside of them? There are only a few places where it is mentioned about something being on their foreheads. One of these is the Shema prayer we discussed earlier. In the passage in Deuteronomy, being obedient to the word is the emphasis.

Deuteronomy 6:4-9 CJB "Sh'ma, Yisra'el! Adonai Eloheinu, Adonai echad [Hear, Isra'el! Adonai our God, Adonai is one]; (5) and you are to love Adonai your God with all your heart, all your being and all your resources. (6) These words, which I am ordering you today, are to be on your heart; (7) and you are to teach them carefully to your children. You are to talk about them when you sit at home, when you are traveling on the road, when you lie down and when you get up. (8) *Tie them on your hand as a sign, put them at the front of a headband around your forehead*, (9) and write them on the door-frames of your house and on your gates.

The scripture says it well. Love the Lord, give Him your heart, teach the word to your children, bind it to your hands (your actions) and put them on a headband around your forehead (your thoughts).

When a priest was anointed for service, the oil was placed on his right ear, right thumb, right big toe and on his head. The oil represents the Spirit, or the anointing of the Spirit. We could simply state that it is a reminder that we are to have the mind of Messiah.

1 Corinthians 2:12-16 HNV But we received, not the spirit of the world, but the Spirit which is from God, that we might know the things that were freely given to us by God. (13) Which things also we speak, not in words which man's wisdom teaches, but which the Holy Spirit teaches, comparing spiritual things with spiritual things. (14) Now the natural man doesn't receive the things of God's Spirit, for they are foolishness to him, and he can't know them, because they are spiritually discerned. (15) But he who is spiritual discerns all things, and he himself is judged by no one. (16) "For who has known the mind of the Lord, that he should instruct him?" But we have Messiah's mind.

His name on their foreheads means that the people have the mind and heart of the Messiah. It also is essential to have the mind and heart of the Messiah to intercede for the people around us. Those with the mind and mark of the Messiah will live while judgment is going on around them in the earth. They will be saved.

Ezekiel 9:4-6 HNV The LORD said to him, Go through the midst of the city, through the midst of Yerushalayim, and set a mark on the foreheads of the men that sigh and that cry over all the abominations that are done in the midst of it. (5) To the others he said in my hearing, Go you through the city after him, and strike: don't let your eye spare, neither have you pity; (6) kill utterly the old man, the young man and the virgin, and little children and women; but don't come near any man on whom is the mark: and *begin at my sanctuary*. Then they began at the old men that were before the house.

We see from Ezekiel nine that it is imperative to have the mind, heart and attitude of the Messiah. The hardest thing to overcome is the battle in our mind. We convince ourselves that all things are too difficult, impossible even. We must tear down all thoughts, imaginations and desires that do not line up with the word regarding us. We must confess and repent for our heart not being the Fathers' heart.

Remember, the Kingdom of Heaven is not something you must wait to see. Stop listening to the lies that we will overcome, someday, by the Spirit of God. Believe the truth that you can overcome _NOW_, _IN_ the Spirit of YHWH! You can live a full life in the Kingdom of Heaven, RIGHT NOW! Be filled with His Spirit and walk in the Kingdom, **today** in Yeshua's name!

Let the refreshing river of life come and wash you and make you clean! He will take you and cleanse you, put His Spirit inside of you, teach you how to walk in His ways and send you out to be a light to the world and healing to the nations.

John 7:38-39 HNV He who believes in me, as the Scripture has said, from within him will flow rivers of living water."

(39) But he said this about the Spirit, which those believing in him were to receive. For the Holy Spirit was not yet given, because Yeshua wasn't yet glorified.

Matthew 5:14-19 HNV You are the light of the world. A city located on a hill can't be hidden. (15) Neither do you light a lamp, and put it under a measuring basket, but on a stand; and it shines to all who are in the house. (16) Even so, let your light shine before men; that they may see your good works, and glorify your Father who is in heaven. (17) "Don't think that I came to destroy the Torah or the Prophets. I didn't come to destroy, but to fulfill. (18) For most certainly, I tell you, until heaven and earth pass away, not even one smallest letter or one tiny pen stroke shall in any way pass away from the Torah, until all things are accomplished. (19) Whoever, therefore, shall break one of these least mitzvot, and teach others to do so, shall be called least in the Kingdom of Heaven; but whoever shall do and teach them shall be called great in the Kingdom of Heaven.

    In the ancient world, the Menorah (candlestick) was referred to as the light of the world. It gave light before the glory of YHWH in a place that would otherwise be dark. It was the only light in the room. He is the only light and life. It is by Yeshua that our light shines within us. If our light is shining, it is Him shining through us.
    Right after He says that you are the light of the world, he says to remember something, you were given the light to spread the word and to live a victorious life in the Kingdom of Heaven. He wants you to remember that your light will shine by keeping the word of YHWH. Do not think that He in any way has come to do away with or diminish the word that was already given. He says that He did not come to diminish the word in your life. He came to cause it to rise up within you and to stand firm in your life!

    As you live your life in the Kingdom, do not come against the mitvot (commands in Torah) that you have already been given. It is worth noting that whoever does not keep the mitzvot, and teaches others to do so, will be called least in the Kingdom of Heaven. Those who keep and teach them will be called great in the kingdom of Heaven.

Life in the Kingdom is life _Now_! You do not have to wait to walk in the blessing of the LORD. I am not talking about having an overload of money. I am saying that walking in blessing is being a river of living water to a lost and dying world! It is being a beacon of light in a world that is too familiar with living in darkness. We are to set the captives free and teach them how to walk in the word and to live in the Kingdom.

Go out and be: Light, Life, A healer, A restorer, A living walking baptism (living water, mikvah), Spirit of truth, Salvation to the world!

Come on in, the water's fine!

NOTES

Chapter Eight

WALKING IN THE BLESSING

To walk in the blessing of YHWH, we must want to receive the blessing of YHWH. This may sound like a no brainer to us. It may come across as sounding very elementary. After all, who does not want to walk in the blessing of the LORD? This is a little more in depth than it sounds.

In order to receive something, we must take it when it is being offered to us. We are being offered the blessing of the Father, but we are not willing to receive it. I say that because, in order to receive it, we must let something go. You can only carry so many things at a time. We fill our hands with all our own pet projects and desires and then end up with no room left to receive what the Father is trying to give us.

One big reason that some believers don't succeed is that they are unwilling to let go. We don't want to let go of those things in our lives that don't advance the Kingdom. If we cannot let go, we may ask for help from a brother or sister in the LORD. Sometimes we have held on to our own things for so long that they are stuck on us. The only way to let those things go is to break them and let them fall to the ground, not to be picked up again.

We need to separate ourselves from this world and it's ways, beliefs and mindsets. Once we are willing to give up the things in our lives that keep us from growing in grace, we will grow in the grace of the One true God. The first thing we need to do is to repent and consecrate ourselves. The Father wants us to be Holy as He is Holy. Since we cannot make ourselves as Holy as He is, we must receive the work that the

Father wants to do in us and keep ourselves from being defiled.

We can make ourselves holy in the aspect that holy means separate. We can and should separate ourselves from the things of this world. By doing this, we have set ourselves apart as holy. So, we do have some part to play in holiness. Righteousness is where we often fall short. If we are unrighteous, it affects our holiness.

Have you ever made a stand for what was right? Have you stood up when no one else would and declared that what was going on was wrong? In doing this, you have set yourself apart in a big way. The problem is, that we then go out and defile ourselves by acting like the world. While we are still in the world, we do not need to live according to the ways and mentality of the world. How set apart are you now? I am not speaking of salvation here. I am talking about being set apart.

Once we are set apart, we need to stay there! How do we do that? By protecting ourselves so that we will not be defiled. Once we have set ourselves apart for the Father, He will show up in a big way!

2 Corinthians 6:14-18 HNV Don't be unequally yoked with unbelievers, for what fellowship have righteousness and iniquity? Or what communion has light with darkness? (15) What agreement has Messiah with Beliya`al? Or what portion has a believer with an unbeliever? (16) What agreement has a temple of God with idols? For you are a temple of the living God. Even as God said, "I will dwell in them, and walk in them; and I will be their God, and they will be my people." (17) Therefore, "'Come out from among them, and be separate,' says the Lord. 'Touch no unclean thing. I will receive you. (18) I will be to you a Father. You will be to me sons and daughters,' says the Lord Almighty."

Leviticus 26:9-13 HNV "'I will have respect for you, and make you fruitful, and multiply you, and will establish my covenant with you. (10) You shall eat old store long kept, and you shall move out the old because of the new. (11) I will set my tent among you: and my soul won't abhor you. (12) I will walk among you, and will be your God, and you will be my people. (13) I am the LORD your God, who brought you forth out of the land of Egypt, that you should not be their slaves; and I have broken the bars of your yoke, and made you go upright.

Ezekiel 37:18-28 HNV When the children of your people shall speak to you, saying, Will you not show us what you mean by these? (19) tell them, Thus says the Lord GOD: Behold, I will take the stick of Yosef, which is in the hand of Efrayim, and the tribes of Yisra'el his companions; and I will put them with it, [even] with the stick of Yehudah, and make them one stick, and they shall be one in my hand. (20) The sticks whereon you write shall be in your hand before their eyes. (21) Say to them, Thus says the Lord GOD: Behold, I will take the children of Yisra'el from among the nations, where they are gone, and will gather them on every side, and bring them into their own land: (22) and I will make them one nation in the land, on the mountains of Yisra'el; and one king shall be king to them all; and they shall be no more two nations, neither shall they be divided into two kingdoms any more at all; (23) neither shall they defile themselves any more with their idols, nor with their detestable things, nor with any of their transgressions; but I will save them out of all their dwelling places, in which they have sinned, and will cleanse them: so shall they be my people, and I will be their God. (24) My servant David shall be king over them; and they all shall have one shepherd: they shall also walk in my ordinances, and observe my statutes, and do them. (25) They shall dwell in the land that I have given to Ya`akov my servant, in which your fathers lived; and they shall dwell therein, they, and their children, and their children's children, forever: and David my servant shall be their prince for ever. (26) Moreover I will make a covenant of shalom with them; it shall be an everlasting covenant with them; and I will place them, and multiply them, and will set my sanctuary in the midst of them forevermore. (27) My tent also shall be with them; and I will be their God, and they shall be my people. (28) The nations shall know that I am the LORD who sanctifies Yisra'el, when my sanctuary shall be in the midst of them forevermore.

Isaiah 52:8-15 HNV The voice of your watchmen! they lift up the voice, together do they sing; for they shall see eye to eye, when the LORD returns to Tziyon. (9) Break forth into joy, sing together, you waste places of Yerushalayim; for the LORD has comforted his people, he has redeemed Yerushalayim. (10) The LORD has made bare his holy arm in the eyes of all the nations; and all the ends of the earth have seen the yeshu`ah of our God. (11) Depart you, depart you, go you out from there, touch no unclean thing; go you out of the midst of her; cleanse yourselves, you who bear the vessels of the LORD. (12) For you shall not go out in haste, neither shall you go by flight: for the LORD will go before you; and the God of Yisra'el will be your rearward. (13) Behold, my servant shall deal wisely, he shall be exalted and lifted up, and shall be very high. (14) Like as many were astonished at you (his visage was so marred more than any man, and his form more than the sons of men), (15) so shall he sprinkle many nations; kings shall shut their mouths at him: for that which had not been told them shall they see; and that which they had not heard shall they understand.

We have often heard that true religion is to take care of the orphans and widows. We are missing the last part of that verse. The emphasis of the verse is for us to do (causatively to be) the word of God! Part of doing the word is guarding yourself from defilement.

James 1:22-27 HNV But be doers of the word, and not only hearers, deluding your own selves. (23) For if anyone is a hearer of the word and not a doer, he is like a man looking at his natural face in a mirror; (24) for he sees himself, and goes away, and immediately forgets what kind of man he was. (25) But he who looks into the perfect Torah of freedom, and continues, not being a hearer who forgets, but a doer of the work, this man will be blessed in what he does. (26) If anyone among you thinks himself to be religious while he doesn't bridle his tongue, but deceives his heart, this man's religion is worthless. (27) Pure religion and undefiled before our God and Father is this: to visit the fatherless and widows in their affliction, and to keep oneself unstained by the world.

In order to receive blessing, we must know the source of our blessing! You must find the source of living water before you can drink it!

Jeremiah 29:11-14 HNV For I know the thoughts that I think toward you, says the LORD, thoughts of shalom, and not of evil, to give you hope in your latter end. (12) You shall call on me, and you shall go and pray to me, and I will listen to you. (13) You shall seek me, and find me, when you shall search for me with all your heart. (14) I will be found by you, says the LORD, and I will turn again your captivity, and I will gather you from all the nations, and from all the places where I have driven you, says the LORD; and I will bring you again to the place from where I caused you to be carried away captive.

We have the promise of the LORD that if we seek Him with all of our heart, we will find Him! So, knowing that He is the same always and forever and that He will not contradict His word, why does He say in Amos 8 that people will seek Him and not find Him?
Here are three options:
1. The people are not His
2. They are looking for something that isn't there
3. They are looking for something else and not recognizing what they are looking for

My belief is that we are a people looking for the blessing of YHWH in all the places where they are not. It reminds me of an old song from the early 80's "Looking for love in all the wrong places."

We must let go of the things that hold us back and move forward into the will of the Father for our lives. We hear so much "well, it's the heart that counts". Gentleman, forget your wife's birthday or your anniversary and try to tell her that your heart remembers but your head forgot. It won't go over very well, will it?

We receive the blessings of the word by being and doing the word. We grow in our faith by doing the word.

Romans 10:16-17 KJV But they have not all obeyed the gospel. For Esaias saith, Lord, who hath believed our report? (17) So then faith [cometh] by hearing, and hearing by the word of God.

Look at what was said in Romans chapter ten. Shaul (Paul) speaks of disobedience and is really equating that with a lack of faith. He also says that faith comes by hearing the word of God. Do you remember what "Shama" means? Shama means to hear, but not just hear, to hear and obey! Faith comes by hearing and obeying the Word!

As we walk in the word it will increase our faith. Faith is an action, not just words. You can say anything you want, but when it comes time to actually deliver, do you really have faith? I have met people who could talk a really big talk, but didn't have the faith to pick up their Bible or to pray. We can say that we have faith, but if we have never had to literally rely on the Father to see us through, we have not shown that we have faith. As stated before, faith is something that has proof of its evidence.

James 2:14-24 HNV What good is it, my brothers, if a man says he has faith, but has no works? Can faith save him? (15) And if a brother or sister is naked and in lack of daily food, (16) and one of you tells them, "Go in peace, be warmed and filled;" and yet you didn't give them the things the body needs, what good is it? (17) Even so faith, if it has no works, is dead in itself. (18) Yes, a man will say, "You have faith, and I have works." Show me your faith without works, and I by my works will show you my faith. (19) You believe that God is one. You do well. The demons also believe, and shudder. (20) But do you want to know, vain man, that faith apart from works is dead? (21) Wasn't Avraham our father justified by works, in that he offered up Yitzchak his son on the altar? (22) You see that faith worked with his works, and by works faith was perfected; (23) and the Scripture was fulfilled which says, "Avraham believed God, and it was accounted to him as righteousness;" and he was called the friend of God. (24) You see then that by works, a man is justified, and not only by faith.

John 10:24-25 HNV The Judeans therefore came around him and said to him, "How long will you hold us in suspense? If you are the Messiah, tell us plainly." (25) Yeshua answered them, "I told you, and you don't believe. The works that I do in my Father's name, these testify about me.

John 14:10-15 HNV Don't you believe that I am in the Father, and the Father in me? The words that I tell you, I speak not from myself; but the Father who lives in me does his works. (11) Believe me that I am in the Father, and the Father in me; or else believe me for the very works' sake. (12) Most certainly I tell you, he who believes in me, the works that I do, he will do also; and he will do greater works than these, because I am going to my Father. (13) Whatever you will ask in my name, that will I do, that the Father may be glorified in the Son. (14) If you will ask anything in my name, I will do it. (15) If you love me, keep my mitzvot.

A really big part of our faith that is missing and keeping us out of some of the blessings for us, is the mentality of "ok I'm saved, now I don't have to do anything".

Ephesians 2:8-10 KJV For by grace are ye saved through faith; and that not of yourselves: [it is] the gift of God: (9) Not of works, lest any man should boast. (10) For we are his workmanship, created in Christ Jesus unto good works, which God hath before ordained that we should walk in them.

2 Timothy 3:14-17 HNV But you remain in the things which you have learned and have been assured of, knowing from whom you have learned them. (15) From infancy, you have known the sacred writings which are able to make you wise

for salvation through faith, which is in Messiah Yeshua. (16) Every writing inspired by God is profitable for teaching, for reproof, for correction, and for instruction which is in righteousness, (17) that the man of God may be complete, thoroughly equipped for every good work.

Titus 1:15-16 HNV To the pure, all things are pure; but to those who are defiled and unbelieving, nothing is pure; but both their mind and their conscience are defiled. (16) They profess that they know God, but by their works they deny him, being abominable, disobedient, and unfit for any good work.

Titus 2:11-14 KJV For the grace of God that bringeth salvation hath appeared to all men, (12) Teaching us that, denying ungodliness and worldly lusts, we should live soberly, righteously, and godly, in this present world; (13) Looking for that blessed hope, and the glorious appearing of the great God and our Saviour Jesus Christ; (14) Who gave himself for us, that he might redeem us from all iniquity, and purify unto himself a peculiar people, zealous of good works.

When we call Him savior, we must call Him LORD! In order to receive the blessings we are promised in the word, we must walk in the ways of the word. We are, in many ways, like the ones who wandered in the wilderness. We need to be told how to walk in the promise that we are about to receive.

We were good at walking in the ways of the world. Now that we have been delivered, those ways are foreign to us. We need to learn a new way to walk. The best way to learn how to walk is to just do it! Sometimes you will fall. You have a loving Father there who will lift you up, dust you off, and put you back on the path. Too often, we would much rather stay on the side of the path upset and refuse to reach out to the Father as He offers us His hand.

The One who created us, knows what's best for us. Have you ever had someone try to tell you how to do your job? What if that person knew nothing about your job and wasn't even in the same field? We have someone who desires to lead us in ways that would benefit us. We think we know a little better about our own lives than He does.

We must come to Him with a heart to know Him. He says that to know Him we must walk in His character (name) and His character is revealed by what He spoke. His word will cause us to know Him intimately. It starts with repentance and a heart to "Shama", to listen and do.

Deuteronomy 26:16-17 CJB

- This day the LORD thy God commandeth thee to do these statutes and ordinances;
- thou shalt therefore **observe and do** them
- with all thy heart, and
- with all thy soul.
- (17) Thou hast avouched the LORD this day to be thy God,
- and that thou wouldest walk in His ways, (derek)
- and keep His statutes, (choq)
- and His commandments, (mitvah)
- and His ordinances, (mishpatim)
- and hearken unto His voice.(shama)

Verse seventeen states that today we have proclaimed YHWH to be our God. Be sure that you make the acknowledgment and declaration that today, He is your God. *Make every day "today!"*

Revelation 12:10-11 KJV And I heard a loud voice saying in heaven, Now is come salvation, and strength, and the kingdom of our God, and the power of his Christ: for the accuser of our brethren is cast down, which accused them before our God day and night. (11) And they overcame him by the blood of the Lamb, and by the word of their testimony; and they loved not their lives unto the death.

Back at verse seventeen in Deuteronomy twenty six, the declaration is followed by obedience to the word. We declare YHWH to be our God and we will...

- walk in His ways, (Derek- way or path)
- and keep His statutes, (choq-customs, manners)
- and His commandments, (mitvah-commands)
- and His ordinances, (mishpatim- judgments)
- and hearken unto His voice.(shama- we will hear and do)

This was not the first time that this was declared, we spoke earlier about Exodus 19 and the people saying "we will hear and do." We must give Him all that we are, heart, soul, spirit and body.

Worship is not worship if your heart is not in it. Worship without obedience is not pure. When Israel brought offerings, it was an act of worship. Obedience must come from a heart of love for YHWH and His word. How does the Father regard worship without obedience?

1 Samuel 15:22-23 HNV Shemu'el said, Has the LORD as great delight in burnt offerings and sacrifices, as in obeying the voice of the LORD? Behold, to obey is better than sacrifice, and to listen than the fat of rams. (23) For rebellion is as the sin of witchcraft, and stubbornness is as idolatry and terafim. Because you have rejected the word of the LORD, he has also rejected you from being king.

In this passage of 1 Samuel, it should be noted that in the original texts, the phrase "is as" is not there. The phrase reads rebellion is witchcraft and arrogance is idolatry. We should check ourselves daily and evaluate our heart and intentions. Surrender them up to the Father and let Him do His work through us as a clean vessel of honor. <u>*Make every day this day*</u>!

Deuteronomy 30:19-20 HNV I call heaven and earth to witness against you this day, that I have set before you life and death, the blessing and the curse: therefore choose life, that you may live, you and your seed; (20) to love the LORD your God, to obey his voice, and to cleave to him; <u>*for he is your life*</u>, and the length of your days; that you may dwell in the land which the LORD swore to your fathers, to Avraham, to Yitzchak, and to Ya`akov, to give them.

Joshua 24:14-15 HNV Now therefore fear the LORD, and serve him in sincerity and in truth; and put away the gods which your fathers served beyond the River, and in Egypt; and serve you the LORD. (15) If it seem evil to you to serve the LORD, choose you this day whom you will serve; whether the gods which your fathers served that were beyond the River, or the gods of the Amori, in whose land you dwell: but as for me and my house, we will serve the LORD.

Jeremiah 40:10 HNV As for me, behold, I will dwell at Mitzpah, to stand before the Kasdim who shall come to us: but you, gather you wine and summer fruits and oil, and put them in your vessels, and dwell in your cities that you have taken.

Jeremiah 44:23 HNV Because you have burned incense, and because you have sinned against the LORD, and have not obeyed the voice of the LORD, nor walked in his law, nor in his statutes, nor in his testimonies; therefore this evil is happened to you, as it is this day.

Matthew 6:11 HNV Give us today our daily bread.

As we understand the concept of "this day" we understand that it means choosing to live today and every day to come, for the glory and honor of YHWH. We honor Him when we keep His word. There are many examples of you being equipped to keep the word. We have seen some. Another is in Deuteronomy twenty seven.

Deuteronomy 27:1-10 HNV Moshe and the elders of Yisra'el commanded the people, saying, Keep all the mitzvah which I command you this day. (2) It shall be on the day when you shall pass over the Yarden to the land which the LORD your God gives you, that you shall set yourself up great stones, and plaster them with plaster: (3) and you shall write on them all the words of this law, when you are passed over; that you may go in to the land which the LORD your God gives you, a land flowing with milk and honey, as the LORD, the God of your fathers, has promised you. (4) It shall be, when you are passed over the Yarden, that you shall set up these stones, which I command you this day, in Mount `Eval, and you shall plaster them with plaster. (5) There shall you build an altar to the LORD your God, an altar of stones: you shall lift up no iron [tool] on them. (6) You shall build the altar of the LORD your God of uncut stones; and you shall offer burnt offerings thereon to the LORD your God: (7) and you shall sacrifice shalom offerings, and shall eat there; and you shall rejoice before the LORD your God. (8) You shall write on the stones all the words of this law very plainly. (9) Moshe and the Kohanim the Levites spoke to all Yisra'el, saying, Keep silence, and listen, Yisra'el: this day you are become the people of the LORD your God. (10) You shall therefore obey the voice of the LORD your God, and do his mitzvot and his statutes, which I command you this day.

Moses and the priests told the people to keep the word they have been given as they enter the land. When they get over the river, they will be stepping foot into the promise of their forefathers. As they are entering the promise, they will have a representation of themselves, standing as a witness for them.

They are to take stones and cover them with plaster. This represents you, the living stones, that Peter talked about. On those living stones will be written the Torah of YHWH! After the stones are put up, they are to take more stones and build an altar, offer peace offerings and be joyful to Him!

1 Peter 2:3-10 HNV if indeed you have tasted that the Lord is gracious: (4) coming to him, a living stone, rejected indeed by men, but chosen by God, precious. (5) You also, as living stones, are built up as a spiritual house, to be a holy priesthood, to offer up spiritual sacrifices, acceptable to God through Yeshua the Messiah. (6) Because it is contained in Scripture, "Behold, I lay in Tziyon a chief cornerstone, chosen, and precious: He who believes in him will not be disappointed." (7) For you who believe therefore is the honor, but for those who are disobedient, "The stone which the builders rejected, has become the chief cornerstone," (8) and, "a stone of stumbling, and a rock of offense." For they stumble at the word, being disobedient, to which also they were appointed. (9) But you are a chosen race, a royal priesthood, a holy nation, a people for God's own possession, that you may proclaim the excellence of him who called you out of darkness into his marvelous light: (10) who in time past were no people, but now are God's people, who had not obtained mercy, but now have obtained mercy.

Revelation 2:16-17 KJV Repent; or else I will come unto thee quickly, and will fight against them with the sword of my mouth. (17) He that hath an ear, let him hear what the Spirit saith unto the churches; To him that overcometh will I give to eat of the hidden manna, and will give him a white stone, and in the stone a new name written, which no man knoweth saving he that receiveth [it].

As they went into the land (the promise) they were to affirm the covenant in the land (the promise). As they were walking in the promise, they were cautioned not to forget the covenant and to walk according to it. In this affirmation of covenant, all the tribes of Israel, and all of those who were joined with them (grafted in), were involved. The covenant of YHWH is for all who would come to Him. Deuteronomy chapters twenty six through twenty eight give us a plain, easy to understand idea of what it means to walk blessed.

We are a people who do what we want and then when it all hits the fan, we look upward to the sky and question the Father as to why He is being so mean to us. We fail to realize that a lot of what we go through, is the very simple process of reaping what we sow. If we sow to life and the things of the Spirit, we will reap Spirit and life. If we sow to the ways, ideas and mindsets of this world, we will reap the ways of this world which lead to death.

We are a society where people have grown up either not realizing or not accepting responsibility for their own actions. The word of YHWH will cause us to see the consequences of our actions (good and bad) and shows us that we will reap them.

Deuteronomy 29:18-21 HNV lest there should be among you man, or woman, or family, or tribe, whose heart turns away this day from the LORD our God, to go to serve the gods of those nations; lest there should be among you a root that bears gall and wormwood; (19) and it happen, when he hears the words of this curse, that he bless himself in his heart, saying, I shall have shalom, though I walk in the stubbornness of my heart, to destroy the moist with the dry. (20) The LORD will not pardon him, but then the anger of the LORD and his jealousy will smoke against that man, and all the curse that is written in this book shall lie on him, and the LORD will blot out his name from under the sky. (21) The LORD will set him apart to evil out of all the tribes of Yisra'el, according to all the curses of the covenant that is written in this scroll of the Torah.

We say in our minds that "God knows my heart." This is part of the problem, He does know our heart. We tell ourselves that we don't need to live the way that He has planned for us and we still expect to be rewarded for it. We tell ourselves that it's OK to sin because we will be forgiven anyway. What a perversion of grace!

If we do sin, we have an advocate for us. Yeshua our Savior will stand and testify of the atonement that He has provided for us. The key to this is having the Father's heart and not running to willful disobedience. To keep this point in front of Israel, they were to establish the covenant in the land.

Deuteronomy 27:9-13 HNV Moshe and the Kohanim the Levites spoke to all Yisra'el, saying, Keep silence, and listen, Yisra'el: this day you are become the people of the LORD your God. (10) You shall therefore obey the voice of the LORD your God, and do his mitzvot and his statutes, which I command you this day. (11) Moshe charged the people the same day, saying, (12) These shall stand on Mount Gerizim to bless the people, when you are passed over the Yarden: Shim`on, and Levi, and Yehudah, and Yissakhar, and Yosef, and Binyamin. (13) These shall stand on Mount `Eval for the curse: Re'uven, Gad, and Asher, and Zevulun, Dan, and Naftali.

The word is full of word pictures and rich in imagery. As the declarations were to be made, they were to stand on two mountains. These mountains were Gerizim and Ebal with the city of Shechem in between them. It's worth paying attention to something here. This still stands as a witness to what happened there so many years ago.

Half of the tribes were to stand on Mt. Gerizim and declare the blessings of the covenant. Gerizim today is a beautiful mountain with greenery and trees. The word Gerizim means to cut up. The word for covenant is brit which means to cut. In both, you will see that the emphasis is something being cut. On this Mountain, the declaration of blessing was cut into the Earth, as well as the heart.

The other half of the tribes were to stand on Mt. Ebal and declare the curses in the covenant. Even today, Mt. Ebal is barren, rocky and not much grows on it. The word Ebal means to make bald or bare. This does testify of the curses contained here, they were for the one who removes himself from under the covering of the Father thus making himself "bald".

The city of Shechem was in between these two mountains. Shechem means neck, as in between the shoulders. A place of decision you could say. I remember as a child watching the old cartoons where someone is being tempted by a devil on their shoulder and on the other shoulder would be an angel telling them not to succumb to the temptation. This really is a similar concept. As the Levites stood between the mountains they were to read declarations from the covenant. As the declarations were read, all of the people were to respond "amen". What a wonderful picture! They knew the names of these places and would understand the imagery that was being shown here.

It goes a little further. All of these people would have spoken Hebrew and would have understood the names of the places. Oftentimes, when you see a place named in Scripture, it is to help us understand what happened there. A person's name was not much different. His name testified of His character. What that person was called was a testimony of that person. This is used in scripture many times.

One example is, when the angel appeared to Mary and explained what was about to happen to her, that she would have a son. One of the names he said that her son would be called was "Emmanuel", which means God with us. His name testified of who He is. He was called "Yeshua" which means Salvation (speaking of the salvation from YHWH). If we understand this, we can understand a little more of the story here at the mountain.

Let's look at which tribes stood on which mountain and the meaning of their names. On Gerizim (cut up) stood: Simeon, Levi, Judah, Issachar, Joseph and Benjamin. On Ebal (barren) stood: Reuben, Gad, Asher, Zebulun, Dan and Naphtali. All those who stood on Gerizim were children of Leah and Rachel, free women. Those who stood on Ebal were children of Bilhah and Zilpah bondwomen (servants), with the exception of Reuben who lost his birthright due to his lust.

- Gerizim – cut up
- Simeon, שִׁמְעוֹן -hearing
- Levi, לוִי -attached
- Judah, יְהוּדָה -celebrated, praised
- Issachar, יִשָּׂשכר -he will bring reward
- Joseph, יוֹסֵף -let him add
- Benjamin, בִּנְיָמִין -son of the right hand (strength or promise)

When all of these names are put together, they tell a little more about the story.

Gerizim, the covenant blessing, is for he who is hearing (shma). He will be attached to this covenant and he will celebrate and praise YHWH because YHWH will bring reward and let him add us as sons of the right hand (strength or promise).

What an amazing declaration of the covenant! To help finish the picture we will look at the other side of the declaration from Mt. Ebal.

- Ebal - to make bald or bare
- Reuben, רְאוּבֵן -see a son
- Gad, גָד - a troop, attack

- Asher, אשר -happy, straight

- Zebulun, זבלון -habitation

- Dan, דן -judge

- Naphtali, נפתלי -wrestling, struggle

Ebal, one who is made bare or has no covering, is a son who is under attack. In order to make happy or straight his habitation (dwelling), he must judge his wrestling or struggle.

When we are wrestling or struggling with the things in life, we should judge (discern) ourselves to make sure that we are not struggling against the Father. We should learn to discern the word of YHWH to see if we are doing anything that would allow a curse to come into our lives.

In order to walk in the blessing of the Father, it all comes down to one word, obedience. We have the provision of the word working on our behalf, if we are obedient to the word. After we examine ourselves and we are obedient, then we can examine other avenues where we feel our spiritual walk is a struggle.

Torah is not a curse! It does however, point out the curse. Curses come in when we transgress the word of the Father.

Proverbs 26:2 KJV As the bird by wandering, as the swallow by flying, so the curse causeless shall not come.

We would be walking in curses ignorant of how or why they are there if we did not have the whole word of YHWH, including the Torah. It is in the Torah that we understand what sin is, because Torah defines sin.

Could <u>some</u> of the troubles we are going through be a result of our rebellion or disobedience? What could we really expect to walk in if we are walking outside the will of YHWH? His word reveals His heart, His will for our lives. Is that something that is bad or negative?

Romans 7:7 HNV What shall we say then? Is the law sin? May it never be! However, I wouldn't have known sin, except through the law. For I wouldn't have known coveting, unless the law had said, "You shall not covet."

1 John 3:4 CJB Everyone who keeps sinning is violating Torah -- indeed, sin is violation of Torah.

Romans 7:12-16 CJB So the Torah is holy; that is, the commandment is holy, just and good. (13) Then did something good become for me the source of death? Heaven forbid! Rather, it was sin working death in me through something good, so that sin might be clearly exposed as sin, so that sin through the commandment might come to be experienced as sinful beyond measure. (14) For we know that the Torah is of the Spirit; but as for me, I am bound to the old nature, sold to sin as a slave. (15) I don't understand my own behavior -- I don't do what I want to do; instead, I do the very thing I hate! (16) Now if I am doing what I don't want to do, I am agreeing that the Torah is good.

1 Timothy 1:6-8 HNV from which things some, having missed the mark, have turned aside to vain talking; (7) desiring to be teachers of the Torah, though they understand neither what they say, nor about what they strongly affirm. (8) But we know that the Torah is good, if a man uses it lawfully,

Throughout the word, obedience to the word of YHWH is emphasized.

Deuteronomy 27:1 HNV Moshe and the elders of Yisra'el commanded the people, saying, Keep all the mitzvah which I command you this day.

In this verse in Deuteronomy, we are told to keep all the commandments or commands that were given. This however, literally reads keep all the <u>command</u>. The word used for command is mitzvah the singular form of the word, not mitzvot, the plural form of the word. We cannot pick and choose which part of the word we will decide to obey. When the word is received, we are to receive them all. We are not coming to the Father picking off of a menu of items.

James 1:22-25 HNV But be doers of the word, and not only hearers, deluding your own selves. (23) For if anyone is a hearer of the word and not a doer, he is like a man looking at his natural face in a mirror; (24) for he sees himself, and goes away, and immediately forgets what kind of man he was. (25) But he who looks into the perfect Torah of freedom, and continues, not being a hearer who forgets, but a doer of the work, this man will be blessed in what he does.

James 4:10-12 HNV Humble yourselves in the sight of the Lord, and he will exalt you. (11) Don't speak against one another, brothers. He who speaks against a brother and judges his brother, speaks against the law and judges the law. But if you judge the law, you are not a doer of the law, but a judge. (12) Only one is the lawgiver, who is able to save and to destroy. But who are you to judge another?

James 4:17 HNV To him therefore who knows to do good, and doesn't do it, to him it is sin.

So, we go back to the mountains. We are familiar with the ten commandments given at Sinai. We take those as they were given and claim them for blessing, as rules to live by, or even a moral code. Yeshua said that if you are keeping the two commandments you will be fulfilling the ten. This does not mean to only do these two things and you will be alright. It means that if you are doing these two things, all of the others will fall in line with them.

Matthew 22:36-40 HNV   "Rabbi, which is the greatest mitzvah in the Torah?" (37) Yeshua said to him, "'You shall love the Lord your God with all your heart, with all your soul, and with all your mind.' (38) This is the first and great mitzvah. (39) A second likewise is this, 'You shall love your neighbor as yourself.' (40) The whole Torah and the Prophets depend on these two mitzvot."

Now we go to Gerizim, Ebal and the declarations. What are some of the things that we may be doing that will allow a doorway for cursing in our life?

Deuteronomy 27:14-26 HNV The Levites shall answer, and tell all the men of Yisra'el with a loud voice, (15) Cursed be the man who makes an engraved or molten image, an abomination to the LORD, the work of the hands of the craftsman, and sets it up in secret. All the people shall answer and say, Amein. (16) Cursed be he who sets light by his father or his mother. All the people shall say, Amein. (17) Cursed be he who removes his neighbor's landmark. All the people shall say, Amein. (18) Cursed be he who makes the blind to wander out of the way. All the people shall say, Amein. (19) Cursed be he who wrests the justice [due] to the foreigner, fatherless, and widow. All the people shall say, Amein. (20) Cursed be he who lies with his father's wife, because he has uncovered his father's skirt. All the people shall say, Amein. (21) Cursed be he who lies with any manner of animal. All the people shall say, Amein. (22) Cursed be he who lies with his sister, the daughter of his father, or the daughter of his mother. All the people shall say, Amein. (23) Cursed be he who lies with his mother-in-law. All the people shall say, Amein. (24) Cursed be he who strikes his neighbor in secret. All the people shall say, Amein. (25) Cursed be he who takes a bribe to kill an innocent person. All the people shall say, Amein. (26<u>) Cursed be he who doesn't confirm the words of this law (TORAH-Teaching) to do them</u>. All the people shall say, Amein.

These curses come to us because our heart and conduct do not line up with how we are to uphold the word in our lives. Everyone wants to claim the blessings. The blessings were given to those who were obedient. Once inside the land, the people (our forefathers) set in place the provisions of the covenant.

Deuteronomy 11:29 HNV It shall happen, when the LORD your God shall bring you into the land where you go to possess it, that you shall set the blessing on Mount Gerizim, and the curse on Mount `Eval.

Deuteronomy 19:14 HNV You shall not remove your neighbor's landmark, which they of old time have set, in your inheritance which you shall inherit, in the land that the LORD your God gives you to possess it.

Proverbs 22:28 HNV Don't move the ancient boundary stone, which your fathers have set up.

Proverbs 23:10 HNV Don't move the ancient boundary stone. Don't encroach on the fields of the fatherless:

The inheritance and landmarks that you have been given are the word and covenant of the Father. Fully read the word, the whole word, in its entirety. This is your blessing and inheritance. Don't take parts of it out. There are blessings and curses contained within it. Blessings come if you are obedient. In our obedience, the Father provides protection. In our rebellion, we walk away from that protection.

Be careful to know the difference between attacks of the adversary and the consequences of rebellion. Just because someone is under attack does not mean that they are under a curse. Nor does a trying time in life warrant a judgment of rebellion from your brother.

James 1:3 KJV Knowing *this, that the trying of your faith worketh patience.*

Through our obedience to the word of the Father, we stay under his protection.

Deuteronomy 28:1-14 HNV It shall happen, <u>*if you shall listen diligently*</u> to the voice of the LORD your God, to <u>*observe to do all his mitzvot*</u> which I command you this day, that the LORD your God will set you on high above all the nations of the earth: (2<u>) and all these blessings shall come on you, **and overtake you**,</u> if you shall listen to the voice of the LORD your God. (3) Blessed shall you be in the city, and blessed shall you be in the field. (4) Blessed shall be the fruit of your body, and the fruit of your ground, and the fruit of your animals, the increase of your livestock, and the young of your flock. (5) Blessed shall be your basket and your kneading trough. (6) Blessed shall you be when you come in, and blessed shall you be when you go out. (7) The LORD will cause your enemies who rise up against you to be struck before you: they shall come out against you one way, and shall flee before you seven ways. (8) The LORD will command the blessing on you in your barns, and in all that you put your hand to; and he will bless you in the land which the LORD your God gives you. (9) The LORD will establish you for a holy people to himself, as he has sworn to you; if you shall keep the mitzvot of the LORD your God, and walk in his ways. (10) All the peoples of the earth shall see that you are called by the name of the LORD; and they shall be afraid of you. (11) The LORD will make you plenteous for good, in the fruit of your body, and in the fruit of your livestock, and in the fruit of your ground, in the land which the LORD swore to your fathers to give you. (12) The LORD will open to you his good treasure in the sky, to give the rain of your land in its season, and to bless all the work of your hand: and you shall lend to many nations, and you shall not borrow. (13) The LORD will make you the head, and not the tail; and you shall be above only, and you shall not be beneath; if you shall listen to the mitzvot of the LORD your God, which I command you this day, to observe and to do [them], (14) and shall not turn aside from any of the words which I command you this day, to the right hand, or to the left, to go after other gods to serve them.

Deuteronomy 28:15 HNV But it shall come to pass, *if you will not listen* to the voice of the LORD your God, to observe to do all his mitzvot and his statutes which I command you this day, that all these curses shall come on you, and overtake you.

Deuteronomy 28:16-68 HNV Cursed shall you be in the city, and cursed shall you be in the field. (17) Cursed shall be your basket and your kneading trough. (18) Cursed shall be the fruit of your body, and the fruit of your ground, the increase of your livestock, and the young of your flock. (19) Cursed shall you be when you come in, and cursed shall you be when you go out. (20) The LORD will send on you cursing, confusion, and rebuke, in all that you put your hand to do, until you are destroyed, and until you perish quickly; because of the evil of your doings, by which you have forsaken me. (21) The LORD will make the pestilence cleave to you, until he has consumed you from off the land, where you go in to possess it. (22) The LORD will strike you with consumption, and with fever, and with inflammation, and with fiery heat, and with the sword, and with blight, and with mildew; and they shall pursue you until you perish. (23) Your sky that is over your head shall be brass, and the earth that is under you shall be iron. (24) The LORD will make the rain of your land powder and dust: from the sky shall it come down on you, until you are destroyed. (25) The LORD will cause you to be struck before your enemies; you shall go out one way against them, and shall flee seven ways before them: and you shall be tossed back and forth among all the kingdoms of the earth. (26) Your dead body shall be food to all birds of the sky, and to the animals of the earth; and there shall be none to frighten them away. (27) The LORD will strike you with the boil of Egypt, and with the tumors, and with the scurvy, and with the itch, of which you can not be healed. (28) The LORD will strike you with madness, and with blindness, and with astonishment of heart; (29) and you shall grope at noonday, as the blind gropes in darkness, and you shall not prosper in your ways: and you shall be only oppressed and robbed always, and there shall be none to save you. (30) You shall betroth a wife, and another man shall lie with her: you shall build a house, and you shall not dwell therein: you shall plant a vineyard, and shall not use the fruit of it. (31) Your ox shall be slain before your eyes, and you shall not eat of it: your donkey shall be violently taken away from before your face, and shall not be restored to you: your sheep shall be given to your enemies, and you shall have none to save you. (32) Your sons and your daughters shall be given to another people; and your eyes shall look, and fail with longing for them all the day: and there shall be nothing in the power of your hand. (33) The fruit of your ground, and all your labors, shall a nation which you don't know eat up; and you shall be only oppressed and crushed always; (34) so that you shall be mad for the sight of your eyes which you shall see. (35) The LORD will strike you in the knees, and in the legs, with a sore boil, of which you can not be healed, from the sole of your foot to the crown of your head. (36) The LORD will bring you, and your king whom you shall set over you, to a nation that you have not known, you nor your fathers; and there shall you serve other gods, wood and stone. (37) You shall become an astonishment, a proverb, and a byword, among all the peoples where the LORD shall lead you away. (38) You shall carry much seed out into the field, and shall gather little in; for the arbeh shall consume it. (39) You shall plant vineyards and dress them, but you shall neither drink of the wine, nor gather [the grapes]; for the worm shall eat them. (40) You shall have olive trees throughout all your borders, but you shall not anoint yourself with the oil; for your olive shall cast [its fruit]. (41) You shall father sons and daughters, but they shall not be yours; for they shall go into captivity. (42) All your trees and the fruit of your ground shall the arbeh possess. (43) The foreigner who is in the midst of you shall mount up above you higher and higher; and you shall come down lower and lower. (44) He shall lend to you, and you shall not lend to him: he shall be the head, and you shall be the tail. (45) All these curses shall come on you, and shall pursue you, and overtake you, until you are destroyed; because you didn't listen to the voice of the LORD your God, to keep his mitzvot and his statutes which he commanded you: (46) and they shall be on you for a sign and for a wonder, and on your seed forever. (47) Because you didn't serve the LORD your God with joyfulness, and with gladness of heart, by reason of the abundance of all things; (48) therefore shall you serve your enemies whom the LORD shall send against you, in hunger, and in thirst, and in nakedness, and in want of all things: and he shall put a yoke of iron on your neck, until he have destroyed you. (49) The LORD will bring a nation against you from far, from the end of the earth, as the eagle flies; a nation whose language you shall not understand; (50) a nation of fierce facial expressions, that shall not regard the person of the old, nor show favor to the young, (51) and shall eat the fruit of your livestock, and the fruit of your ground, until you are destroyed; that also shall not leave you grain, new wine, or oil, the increase of your livestock, or the young of your flock, until they have caused you to perish. (52) They shall besiege you in all your gates, until your high and fortified walls come down, in which you trusted, throughout all your land; and they shall besiege you in all your gates throughout all your land, which the LORD your God has given you. (53) You shall eat the fruit of your own body, the flesh of your sons and of your daughters, whom the LORD your God has given you, in the siege and in the distress with which your enemies shall distress you. (54) The man who is tender among you, and very delicate, his eye shall be evil toward his brother, and toward the wife of his bosom, and toward the remnant of his children whom he has remaining; (55) so that he will not give to any of them of the flesh of his children whom he shall eat, because he has nothing left him, in the siege and in the distress with which your enemy shall distress you in all your gates. (56) The tender and delicate woman among you, who would not adventure to set the sole of her foot on the ground for delicateness and tenderness, her eye shall be evil toward the husband of her bosom, and toward her son, and toward her daughter, (57) and toward her young one who comes out from between her feet, and toward her children whom she shall bear; for she shall eat them for want of all things secretly, in the siege and in the distress with which your enemy shall distress you in your gates. (58) If you will not observe to do all the words of this law that are written in this book, that you may fear this glorious and fearful name, THE LORD YOUR GOD; (59) then the LORD will make your plagues wonderful, and the plagues of your seed, even great plagues, and of long continuance, and sore sicknesses, and of long continuance. (60) He will bring on you again all the diseases of Egypt, which you were afraid of; and they shall cleave to you. (61) Also every sickness, and every plague, which is not written in the book of this law, them will the LORD bring on you, until you are destroyed. (62) You shall be left few in number, whereas you were as the stars of the sky for multitude; because you didn't listen to the voice of the LORD your God. (63) It shall happen that as the LORD rejoiced over you to do you good, and to multiply you, so the LORD will rejoice over you to cause you to perish, and to destroy you; and you shall be plucked from off the land where you go in to possess it. (64) The LORD will scatter you among all peoples, from the one end of the earth even to the other end of the earth; and there you shall serve other gods, which you have not known, you nor your fathers, even wood and stone. (65) Among these nations shall you find no ease, and there shall be no rest for the sole of your foot: but the LORD will give you there a trembling heart, and failing of eyes, and pining of soul; (66) and your life shall hang in doubt before you; and you shall fear night and day, and shall have no assurance of your life. (67) In the morning you shall say, Would it were even! and at even you shall say, Would it were morning! for the fear of your heart which you shall fear, and for the sight of your eyes which you shall see. (68) The LORD will bring you into Egypt again with ships, by the way of which I said to you, You shall see it no more again: and there you shall sell yourselves to your enemies for bondservants and for bondmaids, and no man shall buy you.

Deuteronomy 28:45-48 HNV All these curses shall come on you, and shall pursue you, and overtake you, until you are destroyed; because you didn't listen to the voice of the LORD your God, to keep his mitzvot and his statutes which he commanded you: (46) and they shall be on you for a sign and for a wonder, and on your seed forever. (47) Because you didn't serve the LORD your God with joyfulness, and with gladness of heart, by reason of the abundance of all things; (48) therefore shall you serve your enemies whom the LORD shall send against you, in hunger, and in thirst, and in nakedness, and in want of all things: and he shall put a yoke of iron on your neck, until he have destroyed you.

We do not like to hear anything that makes us uncomfortable.
If it makes us uncomfortable, we think that it must not be God. We say to ourselves "I am a good person. I can do what I please and God will bless me in whatever I do."

Jeremiah 2:35 HNV Yet you said, I am innocent; surely his anger is turned away from me. Behold, I will enter into judgment with you, because you say, I have not sinned.

Deuteronomy 29:19-21 HNV and it happen, when he hears the words of this curse, that he bless himself in his heart, saying, I shall have shalom, though I walk in the stubbornness of my heart, to destroy the moist with the dry. (20) The LORD will not pardon him, but then the anger of the LORD and his jealousy will smoke against that man, and all the curse that is written in this book shall lie on him, and the LORD will blot out his name from under the sky. (21) The LORD will set him apart to evil out of all the tribes of Yisra'el, according to all the curses of the covenant that is written in this scroll of the Torah.

A pure heart and a right relationship with the Father is and always has been the message of the Torah! The idea of a circumcised heart did not originate in the New Testament. It was a Torah principle.

Leviticus 26:40-42 HNV "If they confess their iniquity, and the iniquity of their fathers, in their trespass which they trespassed against me, and also that, because they walked contrary to me, (41) I also walked contrary to them, and brought them into the land of their enemies: if then their uncircumcised heart is humbled, and they then accept the punishment of their iniquity; (42) then I will remember my covenant with Ya`akov; and also my covenant with Yitzchak, and also my covenant with Avraham; and I will remember the land.

Deuteronomy 10:15-17   Only Adonai took enough pleasure in your ancestors to love them and choose their descendants after them -- yourselves -- above all peoples, as he still does today. (16) Therefore, circumcise the foreskin of your heart; and don't be stiffnecked any longer! (17) For Adonai your God is God of gods and Lord of lords, the great, mighty and awesome God, who has no favorites and accepts no bribes.
Deuteronomy 30:6-16 HNV   The LORD your God will circumcise your heart, and the heart of your seed, to love the LORD your God with all your heart, and with all your soul, that you may live. (7) The LORD your God will put all these curses on your enemies, and on those who hate you, who persecuted you. (8) You shall return and obey the voice of the LORD, and do all his mitzvot which I command you this day. (9) The LORD your God will make you plenteous in all the work of your hand, in the fruit of your body, and in the fruit of your livestock, and in the fruit of your ground, for good: for the LORD will again rejoice over you for good, as he rejoiced over your fathers; (10) if you shall obey the voice

of the LORD your God, to keep his mitzvot and his statutes which are written in this scroll of the Torah; if you turn to the LORD your God with all your heart, and with all your soul. (11) For this mitzvah which I command you this day, it is not too hard for you, neither is it far off. (12) It is not in heaven, that you should say, Who shall go up for us to heaven, and bring it to us, and make us to hear it, that we may do it? (13) Neither is it beyond the sea, that you should say, Who shall go over the sea for us, and bring it to us, and make us to hear it, that we may do it? (14) But the word is very near to you, in your mouth, and in your heart, that you may do it. (15) Behold, I have set before you this day life and good, and death and evil; (16) in that I command you this day to love the LORD your God, to walk in his ways, and to keep his mitzvot and his statutes and his ordinances, that you may live and multiply, and that the LORD your God may bless you in the land where you go in to possess it.

Jeremiah 4:3-4 HNV For thus says the LORD to the men of Yehudah and to Yerushalayim, Break up your fallow ground, and don't sow among thorns. (4) Circumcise yourselves to the LORD, and take away the foreskins of your heart, you men of Yehudah and inhabitants of Yerushalayim; lest my wrath go forth like fire, and burn so that none can quench it, because of the evil of your doings.

Acts 7:51 HNV "You stiff-necked and uncircumcised in heart and ears, you always resist the Holy Spirit! As your fathers did, so you do.

    We should receive the word into our hearts like good ground that is being sown for a harvest. Our hearts are much like Jeremiah said in chapter 4:3. In the parable of the sower and the seed in Mark 4:1-20 we see that the harder the ground was, the easier the seed (word) was stolen. Is your ground (heart) hard and stony or is it soft and fertile towards YHWH and His word? The hard stony ground cannot receive the seed and produce fruit.

    When we come to the Father, He cleanses us starting on the inside and then moves outward. In II Chronicles Chapter 29, the temple was defiled and needed cleansed before it could be used in worship to the Father. Hezekiah summoned the priests and put them into service. He decreed that they should consecrate themselves and start cleansing the temple. They cleansed it from the inside out starting with the Holy of Holies.

There are many things in the word that we may not understand because the time for understanding, is not yet here. There are other times in our lives that the word will be revealed to us. These revelations are step by step and they will be revealed to us in the Father's timing. Some things are a restoration issue. There are things in the word that need to be restored to the body of Messiah.

Acts 3:19-21 HNV "Repent therefore, and turn again, that your sins may be blotted out, so that there may come times of refreshing from the presence of the Lord, (20) and that he may send Messiah Yeshua, who was ordained for you before, (21) whom heaven must receive until the times of restoration of all things, which God spoke long ago by the mouth of his holy prophets.

All of these will be revealed at the appropriate time.

Deuteronomy 29:1-4 HNV These are the words of the covenant which the LORD commanded Moshe to make with the children of Yisra'el in the land of Mo'av, besides the covenant which he made with them in Chorev. (2) Moshe called to all Yisra'el, and said to them, You have seen all that the LORD did before your eyes in the land of Egypt to Par`oh, and to all his servants, and to all his land; (3) the great trials which your eyes saw, the signs, and those great wonders: (4) but the LORD has not given you a heart to know, and eyes to see, and ears to hear, to this day.

Isaiah 6:9-10 HNV He said, "Go, and tell this people, 'You hear indeed, but don't understand; and you see indeed, but don't perceive.' (10) Make the heart of this people fat. Make their ears heavy, and shut their eyes; lest they see with their eyes, and hear with their ears, and understand with their heart, and turn again, and be healed."

Matthew 13:13-17 HNV Therefore I speak to them in parables, because seeing they don't see, and hearing, they don't hear, neither do they understand. (14) In them the prophecy of Yeshaiyahu is fulfilled, which says, 'By hearing you will hear, and will in no way understand; Seeing you will see, and will in no way perceive: (15) for this people's heart has grown callous, their ears are dull of hearing, they have closed their eyes; or else perhaps they might perceive with their eyes, hear with their ears, understand with their heart, and should turn again; and I would heal them.' (16) "But blessed are your eyes, for they see; and your ears, for they hear. (17) For most certainly I tell you that many prophets and righteous men desired to see the things which you see, and didn't see them; and to hear the things which you hear, and didn't hear them.

Walking in blessing is walking under the blood of the covenant with a heart to be obedient to the Father. Yeshua ratified the covenant for us by the shedding of His blood and by applying it to the mercy seat in Heaven.

Hebrews 9:11-22 HNV But Messiah having come as a Kohen Gadol of the coming good things, through the greater and more perfect tabernacle, not made with hands, that is to say, not of this creation, (12) nor yet through the blood of goats and calves, but through his own blood, entered in once for all into the Holy Place, having obtained eternal redemption. (13) For if the blood of goats and bulls, and the ashes of a heifer sprinkling those who have been defiled, sanctify to the cleanness of the flesh: (14) how much more will the blood of Messiah, who through the eternal Spirit offered himself without blemish to God, cleanse your conscience from dead works to serve the living God? (15) For this reason he is the mediator of a new covenant, since a death has occurred for the redemption of the transgressions that were under the first covenant, that those who have been called may receive the promise of the eternal inheritance. (16) For where a last will and testament is, there must of necessity be the death of him who made it. (17) For a will is in force where there has been death, for it is never in force while he who made it lives. (18) Therefore even the first covenant has not been dedicated without blood. (19) For when every mitzvah had been spoken by Moshe to all the people according to the Torah, he took the blood of the calves and the goats, with water and scarlet wool and hyssop, and sprinkled both the book itself and all the people, (20) saying, "This is the blood of the covenant which God has commanded you." (21) Moreover he sprinkled the tabernacle and all the vessels of the ministry in like manner with the blood. (22) According to the Torah, nearly everything is cleansed with blood, and apart from shedding of blood there is no remission.

Notice that the writer of Hebrews explains that the blood of the covenant was applied to the people in order for them to fully enter into the covenant.

Exodus 24:4-8 HNV Moshe wrote all the words of the LORD, and rose up early in the morning, and built an altar under the mountain, and twelve pillars for the twelve tribes of Yisra'el. (5) He sent young men of the children of Yisra'el, who offered burnt offerings and sacrificed shalom offerings of oxen to the LORD. (6) Moshe took half of the blood and put it in basins, and half of the blood he sprinkled on the altar. (7) He took the book of the covenant and read it in the hearing of the people, and they said, "All that the LORD has spoken will we do, and be obedient." (8) Moshe took the blood, and sprinkled it on the people, and said, "Look, this is the blood of the covenant, which the LORD has made with you concerning all these words."

Yeshua declared and reaffirmed this covenant with us by giving us an example of what He was about to do before being crucified.

Matthew 26:27-28 HNV He took the cup, gave thanks, and gave to them, saying, "All of you drink it, (28) for this is my blood of the new covenant, which is poured out for many for the remission of sins.

1 Corinthians 11:25-32 HNV In the same way he also took the cup, after supper, saying, "This cup is the new covenant in my blood. Do this, as often as you drink, in memory of me." (26) For as often as you eat this bread and drink this cup, you proclaim the Lord's death until he comes. (27) Therefore whoever eats this bread or drinks the Lord's cup in a manner unworthy of the Lord will be guilty of the body and the blood of the Lord. (28) But let a man examine himself, and so let him eat of the bread, and drink of the cup. (29) For he who eats and drinks in an unworthy manner eats and drinks judgment to himself, if he doesn't discern the Lord's body. (30) For this cause many among you are weak and sickly, and not a few sleep. (31) For if we discerned ourselves, we wouldn't be judged. (32) But when we are judged, we are punished by the Lord, that we may not be condemned with the world.

Deuteronomy 30:6-14 HNV The LORD your God will circumcise your heart, and the heart of your seed, to love the LORD your God with all your heart, and with all your soul, that you may live. (7) The LORD your God will put all these curses on your enemies, and on those who hate you, who persecuted you. (8) You shall return and obey the voice of the LORD, and do all his mitzvot which I command you this day. (9) The LORD your God will make you plenteous in all the work of your hand, in the fruit of your body, and in the fruit of your livestock, and in the fruit of your ground, for good: for the LORD will again rejoice over you for good, as he rejoiced over your fathers; (10) if you shall obey the voice of the LORD your God, to keep his mitzvot and his statutes which are written in this scroll of the Torah; if you turn to the LORD your God with all your heart, and with all your soul. (11) For this mitzvah which I command you this day, it is not too hard for you, neither is it far off. (12) It is not in heaven, that you should say, Who shall go up for us to heaven, and bring it to us, and make us to hear it, that we may do it? (13) Neither is it beyond the sea, that you should say, Who shall go over the sea for us, and bring it to us, and make us to hear it, that we may do it? (14) But the word is very near to you, in your mouth, and in your heart, that you may do it.

Romans 10:3-13 HNV For being ignorant of God's righteousness, and seeking to establish their own righteousness, they didn't subject themselves to the righteousness of God. (4) For Messiah is the fulfillment of the law for righteousness to everyone who believes. (5) For Moshe writes about the righteousness of the law, "The one who does them will live by them." (6) But the righteousness which is of faith says this, "Don't say in your heart, 'Who will ascend into heaven?' (that is, to bring Messiah down); (7) or, 'Who will descend into the abyss?' (that is, to bring Messiah up from the dead.)" (8) But what does it say? "The word is near you, in your mouth, and in your heart;" that is, the word of faith, which we preach: (9) that if you will confess with your mouth that Yeshua is Lord, and believe in your heart that God raised him from the dead, you will be saved. (10) For with the heart, one believes unto righteousness; and with the mouth confession is made unto salvation. (11) For the Scripture says, "Whoever believes in him will not be disappointed." (12) For there is no distinction between Jew and Greek; for the same Lord is Lord of all, and is rich to all who call on him. (13) For, "Whoever will call on the name of the Lord will be saved."

Let us all walk in the confidence that we have a loving Father who will lead us in His ways. He will walk with us in the path. We are all coming to Him with faces unveiled and seeing our Messiah as our everything. Let us strive to keep and guard the path in our heart free from dirt and debris. Walk in the light of the word who is Yeshua our Messiah and walk out of the famine in your life!

YOU CAN DO IT!

Deuteronomy 29:9 Therefore, observe the words of this covenant and obey them; so that you can make everything you do prosper.

Ruach Ministries International

P.O. Box 6370

Brandon FL 33508

To learn more about the Hebraic Heritage of the Christian Faith, or for more teachings and resources visit our website

www.ruachonline.com

or email

djones@ruachonline.com

Numbers 6:24-26 HNV
'The LORD bless you, and keep you. (25) The LORD make his face to shine on you, and be gracious to you. (26) The LORD lift up his face toward you, and give you shalom.'

BIBLIOGRAPHY

Complete Jewish Bible (CJB)

Scripture quotations are taken from the *Complete Jewish Bible*, copyright 1998 by David H. Stern. Published by Jewish New Testament Publications, Inc. www.messianicjewish.net/jntp. Distributed by Messianic Jewish Resources. www.messianicjewish.net. All rights reserved. Used by permission.

King James Bible (KJV)

Quotes are from the 1769 King James Version of the Holy Bible (also known as the Authorized Version)

Jewish Publication Society (JPS)

The Holy Scriptures (Old Testament) by the Jewish Publication Society (1917)

The Hebrew Names Version (HNV)

The Hebrew Names Version of the World English Bible (WEB) and is in public domain

Young's Literal Translation (YLT)

Young's Literal Translation of the Holy Bible by J.N. Young, 1862, 1898 (Author of the Young's Analytical Concordance)

Revised Version (RV)

1885 Revised Version

Dictionary

Noah Webster's 1828 Dictionary of American English

Concordance

Strong's Hebrew and Greek Dictionaries, Strong's exhaustive concordance by James Strong, S.T.D., LL.D., 1890

www.ingramcontent.com/pod-product-compliance
Lightning Source LLC
Chambersburg PA
CBHW061644040426
42446CB00010B/1566